# THE TIMES OF INDIA

# THE SPEAKING TREE

Inspiration for the Soul

**THE SPEAKING TREE - Inspiration for the Soul**

Published in 2009

Second reprint in 2013

by
Bennett, Coleman & Co., Ltd.
7, Bahadur Shah Zafar Marg
New Delhi-110002

**Acknowledgements**
We thank all those who have contributed to "The Speaking Tree" column in
*The Times of India* over the years.

Edit, Design, Marketed and Distributed by

Times Group Books
(A division of Bennett, Coleman and Company Limited)
Times Annexe, 9-10, Bahadur Shah Zafar Marg, New Delhi-110002

ISBN 978-93-80942-12-4

Printed by
International Print-o-Pac Ltd.

Price: ₹250

# CONTENTS

# PREFACE

How does one define 'inspiration'? One dictionary describes it as 'a feeling of excitement and enthusiasm gained from an idea', while another says, inspiration is 'a sudden brilliant or timely idea'. At the practical level, inspiration fires man's imagination. It is actually the spark that fires man's imagination, unlocks his true potential and propels him to rare acts of bravery, sacrifice or creativity. In the absence of inspiration, miraculous feats in different fields of human endeavour would not have been possible. Sometimes ordinary mortals, with nothing much to distinguish them, suddenly join the league of big performers. How does one explain their sudden leap into the limelight? The simple answer is inspiration. Occasionally, even an evil deed acts as a catalyst 'for change of heart' as it did in the case of Ashok the Great. The bloodshed in the Kalinga war made the Maurya king abjure violence for ever.

On the positive plane, the Buddha ran away from home on a mission to rid the human race of all suffering, and Mahatma Gandhi vowed to win freedom for India after he couldn't stomach the humiliation on being thrown out of the train in South Africa. Apart from the deeds of great men what has inspired people down the ages is the word — both spoken and written. Nehru's midnight speech in Parliament on August 15, 1947 continues to inspire us. Abraham Lincoln's oft-quoted letter to his school-going son must have transformed many young lives. By the same token, Norman Vincent Peale's bestseller *Power of Positive Thinking* has turned thousands of pessimists into forward-looking successful individuals.

One need not walk the extra mile to seek inspiration. You can find it in books of history and mythology, in the lives of great men, or even in most mundane things. For example, as King Bruce lay dejected licking the wounds of several battle defeats he saw a spider making vain attempts to climb to his web. Notwithstanding its repeated failed attempts the spider did not give up. Eventually, it got to its perch.Inspired by a mere insect's doggedness, Bruce went to battle once more and won.

Such stories are legion as are instances of ordinary people transcending the limitations of their circumstances and excelling themselves in different walks of life. Needless to say, they were all inspired by the examples of extraordinary people or the uplifting words of great men.

The present volume of 'The Speaking Tree' is an anthology of inspirational writing which has appeared from time to time under this column in *The Times of India*. Some of these writings are about such personalities like Swami Vivekananda and Dhirubhai Ambani and Lord Ganesha, the Divine-Being, to name a few. Some of the writings in this book are by Jawaharlal Nehru, Daisaku Ikeda, Andrew Cohen — the spiritual teacher and author. This volume of 'The Speaking Tree' also cites examples from *The Gita,* The Bible and has anecdote from the *Panchatantra,* Hindu mythology and folklore. It is one book you would love to treasure.

# The Hidden Power of Positive Thinking

Nergis Dalal

 or the traveller on the road to spiritual progress, the primary focus is to find his or her highest potential, which may also be called creative enlightenment. In Abraham Maslow's terminology, enlightened people are referred to as 'meta-normal' beings, those who embody the concept of wholeness, truth, simplicity, effortless energy and transcendence. He claimed that living at this higher level meant greater biological efficiency, less disease, better sleep and increased emotional intelligence.

Physical problems also tend to disappear since they were often the outcome of creative frustration. Not that 'meta-normal' people are immune to fears, tensions and anxiety. These arise from genuine problems, not neurotic imagination. Most of all, they do not dwell on the negative.

In Jose Silva's books on mind-control, an important exercise is to learn how to control the words we use and the thoughts we think. Words and thoughts have enormous power on the subconscious mind, especially if there is emotional involvement.

Long ago Emile Coue persuaded thousands of people to start the day by repeating 'Day by day, in every way, I am getting better and better' twenty times. Those who tried it found the results amazing. Silva suggests that after repeating these words, we should also programme the subconscious every day by saying 'Negative thoughts and negative suggestions have no influence over me at any level of mind'. He claims that results have shown that both these things have far-reaching effects on increasing creativity and bringing a sense of harmony and peace into one's life.

All religions concede that there are different stages leading to higher development. It is not possible to jump from the lowest stage to the highest. This shift is what Erikson calls 'a functional change in the functional equilibrium'. Attempts to take a short cut is fraught with peril. Every journey begins with the first step and progresses stage by stage. Buddhist literature advises the aspirant to have a foundation on which to build, a clear view of the path and the goal and finally, practice, practice, practice. To even aspire to enlightenment is a plus sign. The traveller will find the journey itself rewarding, as the narrow self-image expands, bringing insight and sensitivity. A feeling begins to develop of oneness with all creation. Then comes empathy, strength and understanding. Striving towards the highest goal is not an anxious striving. The aspirant learns to love more deeply, to enjoy silence and solitude and to feel secure in himself.

Deepak Chopra in his book *The Seven Spiritual Laws of Success* says that most people spend 99 per cent of their time defending their points of view, wasting energy and nurturing resentment and hurtfulness. He says that if we give up this habit, refusing to get into arguments, fights and resistance, then we gain access to enormous amounts of energy — creative energy that can be gainfully used, instead of being wasted.

We make our own roads, each one of us, and whether we travel freely and joyously or miserable and burdened by ills and sorrow, is up to us. When we gain access to psychic or formative energy, we enjoy a strong sense of well-being, competence and transcendence. Even if the road itself is non-existent, with the power of positive thinking and by exercising our will, we can ensure that the road is formed as and when we walk on it.

In the Buddhist spiritual teachings it is emphasized that before embarking on any spiritual quest we should apply the six great perfections — compassion, generosity, morality, awareness, wisdom and consistency. All these are tested every day in our lives as we interact with families, strangers and friends. Each one increases personal growth and improves interpersonal relationships. Each one transcends opposing forces, dissension and dichotomies, each one helps us on the upward path. Whether or not we reach this highest state is not important. The journey itself is infinitely rewarding.

# The One who Holds the Keys to the Kingdom

## Janina Gomes

t some stage in our lives, we are confronted with questions that seem to have no answers. We find that we are unable to fathom why our lives may have taken a sudden turn for the worse. We find this difficult to cope with. We agonize over the state we're in and find it easier to wallow in self-pity rather than make the effort to look deeper. When we pick ourselves up and take some time to reflect and analyse how we got where we are, we begin to see the light. Sooner or later, we come to discover that God holds the key to the mystery and problems of our life. When doors close in on us and others have to be opened, it is the Divine Protector who wields the key.

Keys spell safety, security and protection. They secure vaults and keep documents that need to be stored, confidential. In the life of the Spirit within us, God holds the master key. It is God who personally secures us.

Some paths lead us to comfort, others make us comforters. It is said that we have to bruise the rose petal before we can keep and use its fragrance. We are also sometimes called to love that bleeds and friendship that weeps before we touch our deepest needs.

With all precious things as well as with the ordinary and the commonplace, we often have to be bruised and go with beaten wings. But, the Divine Comforter is there, waiting in the wings, to lead us through these tortuous paths, to experience the deep joy of daily life.

There may have been periods in our life, when everything seemed to close in on us; when it was difficult to believe that there could be light at the end of the tunnel. There were probably times when we had to wait indefinitely, often in despair. God's secrets and His plans for our life may have been revealed through a long-drawn sequence of events. Sometimes, we are required to weather the storms in our life. At other times, we are given strength to overcome the hurdles in our way and we find we can draw on a kind of cosmic energy within us that links us with all the positive energies of the universe.

The key to living is not given to us on a platter. We have to be seekers and do our part in every divine transaction. Once we know for sure that God holds the master key to our lives, we make an effort to touch base with the divine within us.

Even in the darkest of times, look for that silver lining. The fog of loneliness, misfortune, pain and misunderstanding is gently moved away and we find ourselves in encounter with God.

God is the divine gardener. He keeps us trim and fit for His kingdom by a continual pruning process, which is why we go through afflictions and sorrows. Once we cultivate a divine perspective, things begin to fall in place. We are not taken in by superficial worldly charms. Like the flourishing and verdant trees and flowers in full blossom, our lives are transformed. This transformation sometimes takes time, at other times it happens in the twinkling of an eye.

When we allow God to take first place in our lives, we find that He gives us the keys not only to our present, future and the past, but that he also entrusts us with the keys to other people's lives, especially those who may come under our influence or who have been touched by us.

The past is over. The present is the now and the future is hidden in the now. God holds the key to all three. The divine keeper finally reaches us to our final goals and destiny in life.

# Healing Power of Daily Prayer

Janina Gomes

n today's rushed world, not many people find the time to pray. Even those who do pray are in a terrible hurry. Naturally then, the heart and mind are often disconnected from the words of prayer which are uttered as a matter of routine. Instead of having a heart-to-heart talk with God, we end up merely reciting. So prayer tends to become a superficial and mechanical task that's not particularly pleasing. Unsurprisingly, one often prays grudgingly.

There are many ways, however, of perceiving prayer. Everyday prayer can help us to experience great spiritual heights when our hearts are touched by moments of exquisite beauty. These moments of grace may be rare of course, but they could capture our whole life and lift us from the mundane, giving us fresh insight into all the lows in our life.

Jesus often suggested to his disciples to 'watch and pray'. People who make everyday prayer a habit are those who have surrendered their lives to the ultimate rescuing power of God and who bank on the external, healing powers of the Supreme Being. It is popularly recounted that Mother Teresa's colleagues in India would often not know where their next meal would come from. They would lift their needs to God in prayer, and sometimes as if in miraculous answer, a truckload of food would arrive from a beneficiary at their doorstep.

The power of everyday prayer is boundless: It is a documented fact that community prayer services have worked miracles, especially in healing the sick. One example of a unflinching faith in the power of prayer is the story of St Monica who prayed without fail daily and untiringly — for her wayward son to be redeemed. Not only did her son change for the better, he went on to become a great doctor and bishop in the church. He was St Augustine.

Daily prayer is not restricted to only asking for personal favours and daily needs, though even this is legitimate and good.

One important reason for everyday prayer is to honour and thank

God, even for the little things of life. "We are His servants not only in lofty cathedrals where His mysteries appear to us in overawing splendour and enrapturing beauty. We are His servants also in the field or the workshop, at the desk or in the washtub."

A theologist writer who advocates daily prayer said, "Despite weakness, depression, and weariness, a small shaft is again and again dug by honest labour, and through that shaft a ray of eternal light falls upon a heart buried by the debris of daily life."

Daily prayer is meant to transform our lives — from lives of gossip, trifles and pettiness and greed to a sincere commitment to God, so that even the way we live in, itself becomes a prayer offering.

Norman Vincent Peale describes his encounter with a man confined to a wheelchair who exuded a rare happiness. When he was a child his mother had left him on the front porch while she did her housework. Somehow he got to the edge of the porch and fell headlong, hurting his spine. The accident left him wheelchair-bound since the age of 12. Instead of wallowing in self-pity he found strength in daily prayer. So he came to exude an unusual sense of God's presence and his method of daily prayer was to pray for other people too, by just sitting in his wheelchair, loving them and giving them to God.

Prayer can help us overcome daily tribulation; it can infuse fresh hope and faith in us, enabling us to face every new challenge with renewed confidence. Community prayers bring different people together, united in compassion and altruistic intention. Prayer heals.

# You Have the Power to Change the World

### Swami Omkarananda Saraswati

 ven a little drop of water can support heavy ships and sustain huge icebergs when it becomes part of an ocean. Similarly, when we liberate ourselves from the limitations of phenomenal existence, and obtain oneness with the Absolute, we attain infinite freedom, power, peace, joy and perfection.

The space in the balloon can support all creation, all the stellar regions, all the worlds — it knows and has faith in the boundless space without, liberates itself from the confines of the balloon, and becomes one with the space everywhere. Even so, if man can know and have faith in God, he liberates himself from his own human limitations and becomes one with God. Nothing, at this stage of perfection, is impossible for man. Until this highest stage is arrived at, man can always work towards achieving what seemed impossible earlier, through devotion, faith, prayer and love for the the infinite consciousness.

Everything great is within yourself. Looking at a huge stone, we can remark that therein is a lion, or a deer, or a beautiful maid, or the Greek philosopher Plato, or an Eastern sage or a Western thinker — and we can go about chiselling the stone until that which we have envisioned emerges. Infinitely more true is this of the consciousness within yourself. You can set about working on it, and produce from it a philosopher, or a sage, or a person of infinite knowledge — in short, anything you desire.

Work on yourself and fashion any type of greatness or perfection you envision. Children looking at the snow may see a little house in it, and set about making that house from the snow. Another asserts that there is a toy in it, and begins fashioning the toy.

The third one claims there is a man in it, and starts building up the snowman. Thus, each produces from the snow the image he has in his mind. All the extraordinary qualities of nature that are characteristic of the world's greatest saints are there in you. If not great purity, some purity is present in you. If not endless knowledge, some amount of knowledge you do possess. Though not superhuman patience, a little patience you do command. If not a great and all-absorbing love for God, some love for that which you recognize as the good, or the beautiful, or truth, or God is active in you.

If all in you is not receptive to the all-perfecting divine presence, there still lurks in you something which appreciates readily the things of love, light, beauty, God. Your love, when fully grown, is the saint. When the little faith in you fully flowers, it is the wonder-worker. Your wisdom, when fully developed, is the sage. Love is the power of powers. Love all, at all times, in all circumstances and conditions, and even in the most difficult situations. Let nothing external, or internal, dry up the perennial springs of the silent, unobserved flow of your love for all.

Transformation of our entire inner nature, of our thoughts, emotions, energies, is a wonderful way of acquiring tremendous spiritual powers. When we exceed the animal and human nature, refine, exalt and illuminate our minds and heart, will and inner spirit, we gain the fathomless power that belongs to our inner, self-luminous spiritual nature.

Constant experience of the presence of God endows us with rare powers. The power to remain unaffected by difficult circumstances, the power to rule the environment, the power of remaining peaceful, joyous, unshaken are among the many powers that accrue to us from the practice of the presence of God. Special concentration exercises awaken the divine powers in us.

Meditation unfolds the higher powers of perception and divine nature. *Japa* — constant repetition of the mystical syllables — puts us in touch with the various powers of God.

We acquire the power to live long by deep and rhythmic breathing. We also gain peace of mind, freedom from physical and mental ailments, and get closer to the knowledge of God. When we wish welfare to all, pray for everyone, every creature, and desire the happiness of all that has life and breathes, we find ourselves enlightened, happy, powerful, peaceful and secure.

# Sacrifice: The Way to Success

Swami Sunirmalananda

he Vedas teach us the practice of *yajna* or sacrifice. The *vedic yajna* is not merely the pouring of ghee on burning firewood. It has a deeper meaning, and is symbolic of life's sacrifice.

Every successful life has a sacrifice-story behind it. The greater the success, the greater the sacrifice. A person successful in any field has performed a *yajna*. The ghee he has used is his own fat, sleep, rest, entertainment — all were given up. The fire where oblations were made was the fire of aspiration that burned in his heart.

Everything in nature is sacrifice. A plant's sacrifice makes the flowers bloom. A mother's sacrifice makes .the child grow. This growth, however, is not without hazards; to grow successfully one needs fitness. So life is competition also. To succeed in it, we need to have five important qualities.

The first quality necessary to succeed is inspiration. The positive thing that inspiration brings is goal-orientation. Lacking in inspiration, our lives become robotic. Why do people suffer from depression, frustration, meaninglessness etc. It's all because of lack of higher goals in life. Whatever be the goal, big or small, without the inspiration to achieve it the goal remains far away. Inspiration isn't mere desire; it is desire plus drive. When somebody interviewed numerous successful people from different fields about the secret of their success, they all replied in one voice: it was drive.

The second quality is aspiration. Aspiration is intense longing for the object we desire. And faith in the goal we have chosen that we shall attain it. Aspiration makes the mind concentrated on the goal, and concentrated effort is what yields success. Aspiration is also like the fence that protects us from going astray. The road to success is strewn with numerous temptations. But we should never look back, and that needs tremendous grit and maturity. It is here that aspiration works.

The third important thing needed for success is perspiration. No one ever truly succeeded in life without putting in sufficient effort.

Life is a cosmic sacrifice, and we are part of it. We can never succeed stealthily. The correct amount of intelligent effort is indispensable for any success. You may ask, "Why don't we succeed sometimes though we have inspiration, aspiration and perspiration? Whenever we failed we were wrong somewhere. Either our choice of the goal was not right or our aspiration lacked fire or our effort was like rowing an anchored boat."

The fourth important quality necessary for success is examination. Schools conduct preparatory exams before final ones. We too should undergo preparatory exams. We should study our progress, one-pointedness, sincerity, the correctness of our efforts, etc. Self-examination or introspection brings out most of our drawbacks so that we can overcome them. However, egotism is one big hurdle for self-examination; it says we are always correct. But the person who examines himself carefully is ever sane and secure.

We need the fifth quality of resignation too. Work itself can't bestow results. Do this and you will get this is correct, but there's someone giving what we get. There is a supreme agent. Though we are struggling our utmost to reach the goal we should know that success is not just chemistry: effort+desire=goal.

Effort is *jada* or insensate. Everything is insensate. Self and God are alone sensate or conscious. Again, we are not islands. There are so many factors and forces — known and unknown — working behind the world phenomenon. So we need resignation. We might have been doing everything needed to reach the goal. Yet we should never become impatient. Our sacred books call for *tyaga* or renunciation, which means giving up ownership. We should resign to a higher will.

Sacrifice is needed at every stage in life: to aspire after something, to struggle for it, to examine ourselves, overriding the ego, to surrender to a higher will. Vivekananda remarked, "Tell me how much you have suffered in life, I shall tell you how great you are."

This then is the *yajna* of the Vedas. *Yajna* doesn't simply mean bearded sages performing *homa*. It means a scientist working on his lab, a film director working on his movie, a tree producing fruit. *Yajna* is the definite well-ordered process from inspiration to illumination which leads us to the goal.

# A Letter from a Father to his Little Son

Rajesh Mani

Dear Pranav,

It's been twenty months since you set foot in the world. When I held you for the first time in my arms at the hospital, your tiny hands were twitching and your eyes were shut tight. Your clenched fist reminded me of a science lesson that said to get an idea about the size of your heart, you should clench your fist. I could imagine the little heart throbbing inside you. The eternal miracle of birth. When it was my turn to witness it, I cried.

Before I married your mother, I used to debate one question endlessly with my friend. Which is, "Is it really worth bringing another life into this world?" Especially when terror has become an ugly leitmotif in the canvas of our lives?

When I switched on the TV that night, the question of whether I was right in bringing you into this world haunted me again. This is my attempt at an answer. Call it catharsis.

I feel there are two ways to raise you. One is to wean you on cynicism. Where you'll erect a sky-high wall in your mind and live your life pouring scorn on everything you see. Which is one way of insulating yourself from fear. A kind of indifferent machismo.

The other way is to prepare you to live in this world. I can't imagine the world for you, son. But I can certainly show you the way to live in an uncertain world. Make a pact with yourself. Understand the following early on. Life is precious. And equally fragile. So every day is a gift. Get up early once in a while just to watch the sun rise. Stare at it intently and burn it in your memory. Be aware of every passing second. Look around you. There's a thin stalk of plant finding its place under the sun in a crevice on the wall of our apartment.

Appreciate mother's cooking. Praise it to heavens. Make it a habit

20

to eat together as a family. No, make it a rule. Fall in love with books. Words will transport you to worlds far away. It will also keep you informed and prepared. Follow your heart. The mind can waver but the heart seldom does. Respect your conscience. It's like a post-it note from God.

When you grow up, seek a job you love. As you enter the world of careers and cocktails, you'll get sucked into a vortex called rat race. Don't be overwhelmed. We're all human. But have the courage to step out of it. Nothing will be lost. Some illusions will shatter. Good riddance.

Money. It's important. But it has its place. Don't make the mistake of putting it right on top. Find your love. Hold it dearly. Be a good husband. A patient father. Give your children space to make their mistakes. But hold them when they fall.

Speak up when you have to. Like this occasion. Whether we like it or not, we're living in a democracy. Sure it has its pitfalls. But don't forget the positives too. The real fight in a democracy is between remembering and forgetting. Go and vote. It's your chance to give shape to the kind of society you want to live in.

Be alert. But try not to live in a state of fear. If you were to get caught in a situation similar to what happened and should we lose you, then you will have left us with enough lovely memories for the remaining years. That will only happen if you start living every day like it is the last day of your life. Though it can never compensate your loss, at least we'll find strength in your love for life.

Don't have regrets. They defeat the very purpose of life. Immersed as I am in work most of the time, this letter is also a wake-up call for me.

Love,
Dad

# Sorry, Champ.
# But this, too, shall Pass

### Simanta Mohanty

t the first Grand Slam tennis event of 2009, the Australian Open, one got to see sublime tennis as well as the depth of the human soul in the final that pitted Rafael Nadal against Roger Federer. For the record, Federer lost a classic to Nadal; the match went the complete five-set distance and will, undoubtedly, be a manual for aspiring tennis players the world over. The behaviour of the two champions at the presentation ceremony after the match, however, should speak to the heart of every human being.

As Federer, carrying his runner-up shield, choked on his tears, the pain on the face of Nadal was there for all to see. The latter's body language as he accepted the champion's trophy, was muted.

There have been many poignant and moving spectacles of triumph in sports. That Sunday afternoon at the Rod Laver arena in Melbourne the stage expanded to show us the greatness of the human spirit. Here then were two men, joined not just by sporting history, but by mutual recognition of the effort it has taken to mould themselves into the champions they are. They know only too well the hours of grinding, pounding training that make their routine, day after day.

These are two men who recognize that behind every champion stand many shadows mocking their passion and ability. These are two men joined by deep respect for each other's pain and talent. Boxer Muhammad Ali once said, "Champions are made from something they have deep inside them — a desire, a dream, a vision." Nadal and Federer are two champions who on that stage showed their essential connectedness.

Their rivalry is already being hailed as one of the greatest ever in the game, but that did not stop Federer from weeping openly at his loss. He was not afraid to show his wound to his great rival, to tell him that all his sacrifices in preparing for the tournament had come to naught. He did not keep a brave face. Sans ego, the vulnerable Federer touched a chord in all of us. Nadal not only saw the wound, he felt it.

A Sanskrit *shloka* says, "Just as the fruit-laden tree bows low, so does the accomplished person in humility." Never has one heard of a champion apologizing to the defeated rival for his win. Nadal has done that on a number of occasions. He said sorry to Federer at the post-match press conference and immediately after collecting the championship trophy from Rod Laver. The Australian Open champion may have been young, but he had the humility of the truly wise.

Osho tells the story of a king who asked a *rishi* for a powerful talisman. The *rishi* gave him a ring containing a folded slip of paper and asked him to open it when faced with extraordinary situations, whether of tragedy or triumph. The talisman, the *rishi* told the king, will keep him grounded; it would help him keep his head in any situation.

The king had many occasions to experience the power of the writing on the paper during a long reign. The paper had on it a simple line: 'This, too, shall pass'. Events and emotions in our life stay alive only in our memory. What remains is the one who experiences, unmoved and unmovable, the one witness, the Presence within us. The great drama of the Federer-Nadal rivalry brings alive the power of the talisman's words.

# Sleeping Lions can't Catch Prey

## Vithal C Nadkarni

hilip B Crosby's moment of insight came five years after he started work. The American management expert had begun in the quality business as a junior technician testing fire control systems for B-47 bombers.

"Completely novice, I learned the simple tasks of adjustment and management without ever really wondering it was all being done at all," he recalls in his bestseller, *Quality is Free*. Then he became exposed to the concept of reliability and thought of a possibility he had never dreamed existed: "Why spend all this time finding and fixing and fighting when you could prevent the incident in the first place?" The entire world seemed to think otherwise. It did concede that prevention was desirable but was convinced that it was completely unattainable and impractical. "It was also referred to as a sort of dream along the lines of King Solomon's lost diamond mines," Crosby adds.

Perfect quality therefore appeared to be a mirage, something that kept slipping through everyone's grasp. Equally impressive was the list of excuses — bad carpenters, their tools and all — trotted out to rationalize the failure. This led Crosby to his epic insight: that quality is free. Although it is free from the attributes of intrinsic goodness or badness, quality wasn't free from requirements however. "The first struggle," Crosby wrote, "and it is never over, is to overcome the 'conventional wisdom' regarding quality."

Crosby's 'unconventional' wisdom — that the cost of quality is the expense of doing things wrong — brought him enormous fame and riches. And it also became conventional when it replaced the traditionally negative aspect of quality control with the more upbeat and exacting standard, that of the zero defect performance.

This stems from Crosby's deep-rooted belief that there is always a right way of doing things. A marvellous resonance of this approach can be found in the *Bhagvad Gita*. In the second discourse of the dialogues, for example, Sri Krishna exhorts Arjuna to be united to pure reason, to abandon both good and bad deeds and to act in harmony with yoga, for 'yoga is skill in action (*yogah karmasu koushalyam*).'

Worldly people will have no trouble in accepting the concept of 'skill in action/right way of doing things'. After all, it can make the crucial difference between success and failure of an enterprise. What is harder to accept is the accompanying psychological prescription — non-attachment to the 'fruits' of action or to its success or failure — provided in the *Bhagavad Gita*. This is supposed to be the quintessence of skilful/harmonized action.

Now why is it that our 'chattering monkey minds' have trouble over letting go of the fruits of action? The answer, ironically, seems to be rooted in one of our intensely human attributes — in the ability to plan ahead and also to review the past. Nothing illustrates this more forcefully than the parable of the day-dreaming potseller from the *Panchatantra*. Even before he has sold a single pot, in his mind's eye the energetic potseller is already getting ready to beat the bride he hopes to marry with the dowry accumulated from the transactions.

Ultimately, however, what he gets is not just a shattered dream but a roomful of pot shards. The moral of the story is that beating brides, even in your fantasies, could land you into serious trouble.

The *Panchatantra* reinforces this message with yet another powerful image — that of the sleeping lion into whose gaping jaws no deer shall fly. The Sanskrit proverb focuses on assiduous industry (*uddyama*) with the implied caveat that it must carried on without the distraction of anticipated rewards or punishments.

So the lion must hunt without worrying about missing or getting his prey. And if he only sleeps? He must be prepared to be shot by a camera in these enlightened times. But they won't give him a ready-made 'meal' tied to a pole anymore because of new-found wisdom about the dangers of making wild lions lazy and loutish. And the potseller, too, must sell his wares here and now rather than fly about with a stick, which can destroy his inventory. Crosby's gospels on quality, for all their focus on industry and manufacture, lead on to philosophy. Just as the *Panchatantra*, for all its animal protagonists and capricious human characters, is really about the art of realpolitik. And it makes for extremely interesting interconnections.

# A Blueprint for Living

### Nergis Dalal

o have remained on the *New York Times* bestseller list for 690 weeks is a remarkable record, even in the world of bestseller lists. This is the feat that the psycho-therapist Dr M Scott Peck's *The Road Less Travelled* has recently accomplished. Unlike many self-help or inspirational books, Scott Peck's book offers concrete guidelines, a detailed map plotted with expertise and love to help us all live healthier, more productive lives.

It does not offer happiness as the ultimate goal, since happiness is often an illusory, transient and even selfish condition. The book opens with three poignantly truthful words — Life is difficult. Once we accept this as inevitable, life immediately becomes, if not easier, then at least more acceptable.

To live successfully in this world, the first essential is to understand oneself: without this, we cannot grow mentally or spiritually; we cannot be caring, sensitive parents, lovers, children or friends. We also need discipline: life is an endless series of problems and when we meet the challenge of solving problems without procrastinating, or ignoring them, we become whole and integrated personalities.

As Jung said, "Neurosis is always a substitute for legitimate suffering." Scott Peck provides four basic rules under the general heading of discipline: knowing how to delay gratification; assuming responsibility for one's own life; dedicating oneself totally to truth or reality; learning the art of balancing or flexibility. Learning how to delay gratification is one of the cardinal rules for success and peace of mind. No great achiever, whether in the realm of sports, art, literature or science, achieved success without knowing that the only way to live is to schedule the pain and effort in life first and enjoy the pleasure and relaxation afterwards.

These are the achievers. Others, however, grow to adulthood without ever learning this skill. They are the problem students who will grow into adults who have developed a pattern of failure which can land them into all sorts of trouble, including alcohol or drug abuse. They will never know the joy of finishing what has to be done before relaxing and indulging in whatever brings them pleasure.

To assume responsibility for one's own life is to recognize and deal with one's own problems and not expect others to solve them, and most of all, never to blame others. Without this rule, a person becomes destructive, ineffective and despondent and, what's more, the problems will persist. People who always blame others for everything that happens to them are, in the author's words, 'character disordered'.

The third tool — a dedication to truth or reality — is a very powerful means by which we can chart our progress through life, constantly revising and changing our trajectory as we grow.

"Mental health," the author says, "is an ongoing dedication to the process of truth or reality at all costs." The last discipline — flexibility — is a continuous process of striking a delicate balance between conflicting needs, goals, duties, responsibilities and directions. We must be able to love without being exploited, maintain friendliness without dependence, adjust to changing situations and maintain our poise and equilibrium as we travel through life.

Scott Peck points out that the conscious mind represents only five per cent of the total and that 95 per cent represents the unconscious. "If you work long enough and hard enough to understand yourself, you will come to know that this vast part of your mind, of which you have little awareness, contains richness beyond imagination." This book provides us with a map on which we can learn to draw, changing boundaries, roads, mountains and valleys as circumstances change, fully accepting the current reality before concentrating on what is positive. If we exercise some control over the direction of our lives, then we can expect, if not happiness, at least the satisfaction of living with love and a dedication to what is right and good.

Facing difficulty enables us to reach a higher level of self-understanding; in the process of experiencing pain, we also learn and grow. As Thich Nhat Hanh puts it, "The necessary condition for the existence of peace and joy is the awareness that peace and joy are available."

# A Monk who Inspires
# all to Face Challenges

Pranav Khullar

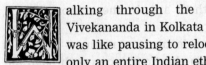alking through the ancestral home of Swami Vivekananda in Kolkata — now a national memorial — was like pausing to relocate the spiritual centre of not only an entire Indian ethos, but deep within oneself as well. The S-spot, the still point, the inner core, was at the centre of his philosophy. Realizing our potential as divine beings, he said, "Each soul is potentially divine, the purpose is to manifest that divinity." His teaching of the universality of all religions, envisioned as different radii within a circle, all leading to this inner centre.

Vivekananda's concept and worship of God was not limited to any one religion or creed, but was radically defined as the worship of the *Virat* itself, the cosmic form of God embracing the whole of humanity at one stroke. Rekindling this Vedantic metaphor of God as *Virat Purusha*, he brought into focus the concept of religion as a universal experience of transcendent reality, common to all and, in fact, underlying all religious faiths and creeds. This principle of the Oneness of the *atman* or Self became the basis for his clarion call for the harmony of all religions at the World Parliament of Religions in 1893.

Aware of the enormous gulf between the concept and practice of this principle, he repeatedly emphasized in his teachings of the urgent need to see and treat every individual as a brother, sister, a fellow companion in our daily lives and not merely dogmatically assert that God is the father of us all.

The idiom of God as *Virata Purusha* was further formalized into a philosophy of service, which has been the cornerstone of the Ramakrishna Order of monks. "*Jiva* is Shiva, this is the gist of all worship, to see Shiva in the poor, weak and the diseased," he thundered in his lectures, by which he would exhort the youth to come out and treat all humans as equal, "...those who see Shiva only in the image, their worship is but preliminary." The road map to Narayana has to be through service to the *Daridra-Narayana*, the poor, the less privileged, the needy and the homeless.

Nirvana was no longer a solipsistic route to personal salvation, but a collective effort to address the basic needs of every person less privileged first. This paradigm has inspired generations since, and is said to have influenced even John Rockefeller after a personal meeting with Vivekananda. He transformed the rest of his life completely to philanthropic efforts. Rockefeller was given to understand that he was only a channel, and that God had given him wealth as an opportunity to help and do good to other people.

Watching the young monks clean Vivekananda's room at Belur Math later one evening — as if he were just about to come in to meditate after a hard day's work — one is humbled by the stature of the monks' efforts in rousing people out of their *tamas* or inertia of superstition and pettiness. Tagore told a group that ..."if you want to know India, read Vivekananda." Such a blazing life of inspiration it was to seekers and thinkers and lay persons alike. His rousing war cry of "Arise, awake, and stop not..." is predicated on the concept of strong, fearless individuals unfettered by creed or caste or social standing. This call to action, to karma above all else, is encapsulated in his own words, "They alone live, who live for others, the rest are more dead than alive." This war cry to arouse the sleeping soul is as critically inspirational at all times, and particularly in the face of today's tremendous challenges.

# Formula for Success in Rooster's Tale

Sudhamahi Regunathan

his is the story of a king who wanted a painting of a rooster to adorn his palace. He sent his messengers far and wide to get him a good painting. Alas! None of the paintings inspired the king. So he announced a competition. Artists from far and wide came with their entries. The king invited an old painter who had taught him as a child to adjudicate.

Many people had gathered in the hall where the exhibits were displayed. The old artist examined each painting slowly and deliberately. He walked back and scrutinized the paintings for a second time. Then, quietly rubbing his chin, he walked towards the king.

"Well?" asked the king expectantly. "Have you made up your mind?"

The artist hesitated. "Why do you hesitate to speak? Please tell me, who is the winner?" asked the king. The judge went closer to the king and announced, "Sir, I do not think any painting qualifies."

A stunned silence followed. The artists expressed their indignance. The king, too, was puzzled. "Are you not being a little too severe?" he asked.

"The acid test would be to let some cocks into the room. Whichever painting they begin fighting with, that can be immediately judged to be the best, as that would be the most realistic. Cocks as you know have this tendency to fight when they see another of their species," said the old artist. Accordingly cocks were brought in. All of them walked past the paintings without as much as turning their heads.

"Can you paint one which will elicit a response from a cock?" asked the king of the judge.

"Sir, I can. But I need six months' time," he said. The king agreed and it was decided that they would meet at the same place six months hence. Six months later, all the artists gathered once again. The old artist, however, had brought no painting with him. The king was perplexed.

"I will paint now, Sir. I just need the materials," said the artist. The king ordered for the paper and the colours. The artist settled down to work and soon his painting was ready. It was exhibited along with the others. Cocks were once again made to enter the room.

All of them made a beeline to the old man's painting and started attacking the cock on the canvas. Indeed his painting had passed the test. "What is the secret? Why did you not paint for six months and instead do it only in the last half hour?" asked the king.

Replied the old man, "Sir, for the past six months I have been living with cocks. I ate like them, slept like them, walked like them — I lived as if I were a cock myself. Only then did I paint a cock."

"It is *ekatmakta* or oneness with the subject that helped him create a close likeness to the cock," says Acharya Mahapragya.

"In whatever you do, there is need to feel oneness with the activity. This is the secret to success in any field. Even when you pray, there is need to feel oneness with the prayer and the one prayed to. When we say *Namo arahant tanam,* do not say it mechanically. Experience it, feel one with it. An *arahat* is an awakened pilgrim. Imagine that those sitting around you are *arahats*, those behind you are *arahats* and you too are *arahat* within. Then say those words which will be full of meaning. Once you feel oneness with the rest of the world, negative emotions will stop plaguing you. You will see an image of yourself in all other beings and be at peace with yourself."

# Think Positive, Reap Benefits

### BK Sushant

n the Mahabharata, when Dharmabaka asked, "Who is a true Brahmin?" Yudhisthira answered, "The one who always harbours goodwill and good wishes for all beings in the universe is a true Brahmin." This is the power of positive thinking — it can bring about welfare for all, create and sustain better quality of life and relationships.

When the Buddha was asked how to sustain a positive attitude towards those who bear ill-will, he answered: "If you don't take the ill-will people intend to inflict upon you, then that remains with them and you stay unaffected."

In two ways a person can remain uncontaminated by negativity: By physically or mentally dissociating the self from undesirable vibrations through practice, penance and austerity, achieving a mental state of detachment and dispassion. The second option is simple: By inculcating positive values like peace, love, compassion and cooperation, by broadening one's attitude, perception and mindset. You have to lift the mind from narrow distinctions of mine and thine, caste, creed, community, race and religion. It also involves going beyond servitude to sense organs and sensual pleasures. It requires self-regulation and self-control over your emotions and passions.

When the mind is peaceful, content and full of positive feelings for all beings, then no amount of negative stimulation can disturb or distract it from its benign state. Even wild animals like lions, tigers, serpents are known to have lived peacefully in the habitats of hermits in ancient times because of the powerful spell of pure and positive vibrations emanating from those meditating sages.

A person with positive thoughts is selfless, fearless and eager to serve, share and sacrifice for the welfare of others. By contrast, persons of ill-will are selfish, fearful, sinful and stressful. The slightest disturbance in their way of thinking and living upsets and even uproots them from their vain and illusory pursuits.

Positive people are strongly rooted in the original nature or qualities or religion (*swadharma*) of the self such as peace, purity, love, wisdom and happiness. Nothing can uproot them from their position of peace, tranquillity and equanimity by virtue of which they remit strong vibrations of spiritual energy, solace, bliss and contentment. The power of positivity is not something which is god-gifted or which can be attained by a chosen few only. Rather it is the innate nature or quality of the self in every human being which can be brought to the fore through proper and regular cultivation and practice of our rich and ancient spiritual knowledge, universal values and divine contemplation or meditation on one's inner self and on the supreme soul. The real source and sustainer of positive and healthy thinking, outlook, values and powers are spiritual wisdom and *Rajyoga* meditation which facilitate and foster the process of understanding and experiencing the holy communion of one's inner self with the supreme soul.

From such daily doses of divine introspection and meditation, eight main positive powers emerge and flourish in the self. These are the powers of tolerance, adaptability, discernment, decision-making, courage, cooperation, patience and humility which are essential to realize and restore holistic health, harmony and happiness in our life and society today.

To reinforce and strengthen these powers of positivity and spirituality as a natural force and flow in one's consciousness, character and conduct, the habits of having holy companionship, godly knowledge, self-control and continence, *satvic* diet and of rendering selfless socio-spiritual services are indispensable prerequisites.

# Subconscious Mind
# is Power-packed

Seema Burman

hen we think of 'me' we think of our conscious mind, the mind of which we are fully aware. This seems to make decisions for us and directs our activities. This part of the mind analyses, criticizes, even commands us. The subconscious mind, however, keeps us going without us being aware of it. Besides, it has the power of memory. It stores information. Whatever we see, hear, smell, taste, touch or feel passes through the conscious mind and reaches the subconscious where it is stored. Even after several years, if we wish to recall a name, an address, figures, the subconscious is at our service. This is called activating the subconscious mind.

There is another part of the mind, the super conscious mind — the creative force which has all answers of the universe. The bright ideas that fuel inventions, that inspire writers and directors originate from here. So do psychic powers, intuition and the sixth sense. We have to learn to use this power for positive purposes.

Scriptures tell us that the enemy lies within us. Who is this enemy? Our very own negativity. How can you get rid of this enemy within? By positive auto-suggestion. But first, turn off that censor in your head; convince your self that your suggestions are true. So instead of saying, "I will not smoke," say, "I am quitting smoking." If you say, "I will quit smoking," the subconscious knows that you will quit smoking in the future. You have to translate what that means — it could be two minutes, two hours, two days, two years. So each time, be specific.

In *Quantum Healing* Deepak Chopra explains, "Psychiatrists see patients every day who are crippled by boundaries, people who have programmed guilt, anxiety and insecurities into themselves. Boundaries  created in silence are the most confining. The mechanism behind phobias can be used in exactly the opposite way, to take down a wall rather than build one."

Direct your suggestions towards what you want rather than towards what you do not want. Instead of saying, "I am not afraid," say, "I am unafraid." Instead of, "I will never be late," say "I will be punctual." Use the present tense. The subconscious is not only obedient, it is dumb too. It does not think on its own, it does not act on its own. Let your suggestions acquire a date, sound, picture, smell — feel the suggestion, visualize it, hear it and repeat it like the commercials. Be authoritative.

For this, you have to improve your self-esteem. You have to repeat to yourself the following, "I love myself; I believe in myself; I will forgive those who offend me; I believe in my family; I deserve the best, I get the best; I believe that success is the result of intelligent effort; I believe in prayer; I believe I will get out of life exactly what I put into it."

"Every thought you are thinking creates a wave in the unified field. It ripples through all the layers of ego intellect, mind, senses and matter spreading out in wider and wider circles. You are like a light radiating not photons but consciousness. As they radiate, your thoughts have an effect on everything in nature.

"Physics already recognizes this fact," says Deepak Chopra. Hypnotists and psychiatrists world over have reported patients carrying psychosomatic problems from their previous lives. A distasteful experience is remembered by the subconscious mind. You cannot get rid of it till you command your subconscious to forget it and start afresh.

Swami Sivananda explains, "Intense passion, hatred, long standing bitter jealousy, corroding anxiety, fits of hot temper actually destroy the cells of the body and induce disease of the heart, liver, kidneys, spleen and stomach. Violent fits of hot temper do serious damage to the brain cells, throw poisonous chemical products into the blood, produce general shock and depression and suppress the secretion of gastric juice, bile and other digestive juices in the alimentary canal, drain away your energy, vitality, induce preventive old age and shorten life."

'You are your best friend and your worst enemy' refers to the subconscious mind's function. 'Nothing is impossible' refers to the subconscious mind's power.

# Forgiveness: Journey to Other Selves

Sitakant Mahapatra

ne of the most important requirements in the long journey to cosmic consciousness — a state when you are one with the universe — is the capacity to forgive. Since all of us sin, we will be incapable of redemption unless we learn to forgive. We can't remove the black stain of sin which only God can. Therefore it is rightly said that to err is human, to forgive divine. As Milan Kundera puts it, "Divesting a sin of its validity, undoing it, erasing it out of time, in other words, making it into nothing is a mysterious and supernatural feat. Only God, because he can work miracles, may wash away sin, transform it into nothing, forgive it. Man can forgive man only in so far as he founds himself on God's forgiveness."

The capacity for forgiving has been beautifully brought out in the Gospel according to St. John, and I can't resist the temptation of quoting it at length: "And the Scribes and Pharisees brought unto him a woman taken in adultery and when they had set her in the midst, they say unto him, 'Master, this woman was taken in adultery, in the very act. Now Moses, in the law, commanded us that such should be stoned, but what sayest thou?' "

But Jesus did not reply, and when they continued bothering him with the same question he said unto them, "He that is without sin among you, let him first cast a stone at her." And they who heard it, being convicted by their own conscience, went out one by one even unto the last and Jesus was left alone and the woman standing in the midst. Jesus said unto her, "Woman, where are those accusers? Hath no man condemned then?" She said, "No man, Lord". And Jesus said to her, "Neither do I condemn thee; go and sin no more."

Besides the capacity to forgive, one needs to develop the capacity of love, compassion and empathy. The journey away from ego-centrism to the cosmic self, which is the essence of all religions, demands that we feel the sorrow of the entire world within our bones. Sometimes this may even result in an apparent withdrawal from man and society. When Prince Gautama left the comforts and luxury of the palace and his beautiful loving wife, he was not running away from the world. In fact he was leaving the world we all prize because he was too deeply in love with man and his happiness and had seen too deeply into the cause of sorrow which was desire. It was thus the highest love that made him renounce the known illusions of life and prosperity. True love makes one a true rebel and Buddha was and still remains the greatest lover of mankind as also the greatest rebel who said 'no' to the prevailing social values. The imperative of the journey from one's limited, self-centred, windowless monad of a self, to a gradually ascending higher consciousness becomes clear when we look at some of the most profound statements on this matter. Teilhard de Chardin put it most beautifully and cryptically when he said, "To be more, one must unite more fully." Your strength, in other words, lies in extending the borders of your awareness, of your concerns and not restricting or choking your awareness to a narcissistic impulse.

When once asked to express in one word the guiding principle of happy life, Confucius replied, "It is altruism." And what is altruism in its essence? It is a total orientation away from selfishness and towards the good of others, to the sharing of joys and sorrows of the whole world. The other becomes the justification for my being on this earth. Albert Schweitzer working for the sick and infirm in African jungles put it this way: "I am life wishing to live in the midst of the lives which also wish to live." Such an authentic and altruistic self becomes possible only when one is deeply aware of one's failings, one's inadequacies. St Augustine put it in a telling manner: *si fallor sum* (I err, therefore I exist).

Inside every man there are various levels of awareness corresponding to the levels of his existence. *Vidya* or knowledge is not information gathered from books or manuals. Our culture defines it as *Sa vidya ya vimuktaye*: that is knowledge or wisdom which sets you free. Free from the narrow confines of ego, from one's own lower or baser nature, from darkness, from the prison-house of selfish desires.

# The Dacoit & the Poet: A Saga of Compassion

Amrit Gangar

n the town of Anjar near Kandla port in Kutch there are the tombs of Jesal and Toral, together known as Jesar-Turi. The legend of how Toral, the saint poetess, changed Jesal, the dreaded dacoit into a simple, saintly man is very popular among local people.

In the middle of the fourteenth century, Jesal had terrified the people of Kutch and its surrounding areas. The story is that when he heard about a fine mare called Tori belonging to one Sanstiyaji, living in the village Saladi in Kathiawar, Jesal was tempted to steal the mare. He was also attracted towards Sanstiyaji's extremely charming wife Torande, who incidentally was also known as Tori. Though leading a wordly life, Torande had detached herself from it and was well known as a saint poetess. The dacoit had no consideration for all this.

Jesal reached Sanstiyaji's village on a *jagran* night when the village folk were busy performing *puja* in the common square. His entry into the stable in the pitch dark startled Sanstiyaji's mare and she ran away uprooting the nail to which she was tied up. She was brought back into the stable by a servant who tried to replace the nail. Jesal had hidden himself under a heap of fodder and the nail pierced his palm. Brave, he faced the terrible pain without uttering a word. Without moving about, he lay there writhing in pain. When the *puja* was over, someone who was distributing the *prasad* heard the screams of Tori the mare.

He went into the stable and found Jesal, with his palm bleeding profusely. The kind man removed the nail from Jesal's palm, treated him and gave him *prasad*. Although Jesal confessed his true identity, everyone was appreciative of his great courage and endurance. It was then that Tori, the saint poetess, decided to try and transform him into a pious man.

Tori tried to convince him through her poetry that the path he had taken was not right. She even showed her readiness to go with him if he changed himself from a dreaded dacoit to a pious devotee. Jesal agreed and they started their journey towards Kutch. On the way, when they were crossing the sea by boat, they were trapped in a fierce storm; the sea had turned mad. Tori saw how the ferocious dacoit was scared of death. In the midst of the sea and the storm, Tori, through her poetry, made him understand the meaning of life and there came a metamorphosis in him.

The poetry she composed is still sung as *bhajans* or devotional songs by the people of Kutch. In the sinking boat she appealed to Jesal: "O You Rajput! reveal all your sins and take care of your *dharma*; I won't let your boat sink, that is what Toral tells you." Jesal was really repentant and he responded to Toral saying, "O you sati Torande my sins are as many as the hair on my head, this is what Jesal tells you." Jesal confessed all his evil deeds to Toral and gradually got cleansed of his guilt.

Their dialogue went on as they sailed towards their destination amidst the deadly storm. Toral, cleverly and affectionately, convinced Jesal that he should shed his past sinful life, and begin a new, austere and pious life. Eventually the storm passed, and the tranquil waters took Jesal and Toral safely to their destination. Metaphorically, Jesal's boat had safely crossed the ocean of life.

Back at Anjar, Jesal spent his life as a saintly person, dedicating himself to prayer and service of the poor. The saint poetess Toral transformed many men from being evil characters into good souls. For rest of his life, Jesal remained Toral's dedicated comrade.

When Jesal died in *samadhi*, Toral also decided to give up her life with him in *samadhi*. The tombs of Jesal and Toral are situated close to each other. People believe that the tombs are moving closer and closer to each other, may be by a fraction of a centimetre each year, and as the popular belief goes, when the two tombs will touch each other, the world will end. Belief apart, what is significant is the strength of womanhood epitomized by Toral, the saint poetess who had the courage and confidence to go with a dreaded dacoit. And turn him into a decent human being.

# Reinvent Yourself, Renew Your Life

### Janina Gomes

hen the primary reason for a person's existence is outgrown or lost, he or she may begin to die, or self-destruct rather than reinvent themselves. Some people end their lives after the loss of money, work, status or a limb, their beauty, their sexuality, or a loved one. This is true of those who believe they have only one way of being that is possible for them, one way to live and be. When the ground or value of their existence is eliminated, so is their existence. Our socialization practices encourage people to believe that they can only be in one way, so that they cannot imagine or invent new purposes, new identities, new lives, when old ones have run their course.

Every human being is challenged to change and to grow from one phase of life to another and to take on a new role, when the old role has ended and outlived its utility. People live as long as they experience meaning and value. They continue to live as long as they have hope of fulfilling meanings and values. As soon as meaning, value and hope vanish from a person's experience, they stop living and begin to die.

Sidney M Jourard, in his work *The Transparent Self*, invites self-disclosure. He links health and personality development to significantly making one's true self known to another or others. He believes that though we expect to live to riper ages than we did one hundred years earlier, we kill ourselves in another way — by encouraging ourselves to believe that there is only one identity, one role, one way for us to be, one value for us to fulfil rather than a host of possible reinventions to be lived in a lifetime.

Jourard feels that mental and physical illness are evidence that the way in which the person has been living up to the point of his or her collapse has truly been outgrown. It is time to stop that way of life and invent a new way that is compatible with well-being. Often, members of the healing and helping professions interpret the distress signals to mean that a way of life has been outlived and view it as an illness to be cured, rather than as a call to stop, reflect and meditate, dream and invent a new self. When projects are outworn, it is time to re-project and not anaesthetize the experience of despair or disinfect the gut, because if the sick person resumes the life that has been sickening him or her, it will just kill the person.

We can train our ourselves to liberate our consciousness from fixations so that through imagination and creative reconstruing, a person can untrap himself or herself from the situation. While society may emphasize a certain narrow role for a person as a productive unit ie, holding a place in society only to create wealth and goods, religion emphasizes the uniqueness of God-given qualities endowed to each individual to create a unique and irreplaceable personal destiny.

Jourard believes that people should be taught a spiritual theory of personal growth that encourages them to let a certain role die, without killing their embodied selves, so that they can invent new ones and find places and company to live them until they die of being worn out. He feels meditation and retreat centres, rather than hospitals, where the invitation to live is seriously extended and where guides are available to help a person change the identity that he has outgrown so he can invent a new one — these may be an answer to the problem of self-destruction. For example, a retired manager or executive may find a new role as a social worker by engaging in humanitarian work.

In life, religion helps us to go from one stage of life to another smoothly. When threatened by cruel circumstances and crises, it helps to create a strong identity which sustains the person through these. When one way of life has outlived its utility or has been finished, it helps us to find a new identity and a new role.

To continue with an outlived role is an invitation to die, whereas to reinvent oneself and create new meaning is to find a new meaning and value in life. Awareness is the key to human consciousness. Those who experience life with greater intensity, have more awareness. Those who would seek to diminish our awareness are creating blocks to the free flow of life. In the quest for wholeness, we may have to create and live many lives in our earth-bound existence.

# Lose & Still be a Winner

## KS Ram

alph Emerson, the 20th century American philosopher, described man as the 'ever-losing winner'. We tend to measure God's blessings on the basis of how many of our prayers have been answered — we compare what we sought with what we got. We do not often get what we prayed for. Then we accuse God of being unkind. Subsequently, we discover later that whatever happened was in fact for the good. The 'bad' event turns out to be a blessing in disguise.

Rabindranath Tagore in *Gitanjali* thanks God for the various denials in life. "My desires are many and my cry is pitiful, but ever didst thou save me by hard refusals; and this strong mercy has been wrought into my life through and through." Can anyone ever pray to God for self-damaging things? Indian thought explains this through two terms — *preyas* (the pleasant) and *shreyas* (the good). Whatever is pleasant may or may not be ultimately good. We are quick to know what is pleasant, but not what is good. If we are guided by our senses, we may pursue *preyas*, mistaking it for *shreyas*. God understands what is good for us better than we ever can. When he denies our most earnest prayer, he, in fact, is being merciful to us.

The story of Narada's infatuation rendered by Tulsidas in his *Ramcharitmanas* illustrates this point. This story occurs in the context of Narada's curse to Narayana (Balakanda, 124-137). Narada became vain when he defeated Kama, the God of Love, although he achieved this by the grace of God. The Lord resolved to set the record straight. A magic city was designed with Shilanidhi as its king. Vishwamohini, his daughter, had to choose her groom. Narada walked into the king's palace and was reverently greeted by the king who called the princess to the *muni's* presence.

When he beheld the beautiful princess, Narada was overwhelmed and began to cherish the thought of marrying her. Losing his spiritual equilibrium under a sensual spell, he thought: "This is no time for prayers. What is needed on this occasion is great charm and personal beauty, so that the princess may be charmed when she sees me and cast upon me the garland of victory!" Hard-pressed for time, he, however, invoked the Lord and prayed: "Right speedily do that which may serve my best interests, for I am your own servant, O Lord!" The Lord forthwith granted Narada's prayer.

Narada was sure the princess was now his and none other's. While Narada sat at the *swayamvara* of the princess, excitedly trying to catch her attention, the girl saw him through the design of God as a hideous monkey. In great indignation, she did not so much as glance Narada's way. Narada was furious. Advised by two jeering attendants to go and see his face in a mirror, Narada saw his hideous face and felt that the Lord had deceived him and cursed the Lord in a fit of anger.

The Lord, however, had done what he had promised to do: ensure the good (*shreyas*) of his devotee. The great sage had erred in desiring for the pleasant; the Lord frustrated his desire by doing what was good for him. We are all like Narada: the 'ever-losing winner'.

Coming to the subject of prayer: What should we pray for if we are incapable of discriminating the good from the pleasant? The answer is: Nothing, except God's grace. Jesus advises his followers (Matthew 6:8-10): "Your Father knoweth what things ye have need of, before ye ask him." His prayer therefore is: "Our father... thy will be done!" That is, may your (not my) will be done!

# Leadership Qualities in Vighneshwara

## Swami Swaroopananda

anesha, the elephant-headed God, combines within himself all the essential qualities of a successful leader. *Pati* means master or leader. *Gana* stands for the attendants. Hence He is also called Vinayaka, the supreme leader of the *ganas*, one who attends upon and follows at all times Lord Shiva. He is also Vighneshwara, Lord of all obstacles.

Ganapati has two spouses: Buddhi or intellect and Siddhi or achievement. Ganesha represents perfect leadership. He is the possessor of perfect wisdom — a fully realized being. To a student of Vedanta, the 'path of knowledge' is the prescribed path, which is essentially intellectual. So, a leader must have a 'great head' to conceive and understand the logic of spiritual thought. The truth of Vedanta can be comprehended only through listening to a teacher. Therefore, *shravanam* or listening is depicted by Ganapati's large ears. Difficult and thorny issues are resolved by intelligent listening. Quarrels and conflicts come up in an organization, at the workplace, or in the family — all because no one is ready to listen. After listening, the individual must independently reflect (*manana*) upon what he has heard. For this he needs to be sensitive enough to be aware of all creatures. His intellect must have the depth and width to understand the entire world of plurality. He must have the subtle discriminative power, *viveka*, to distinguish the changing perishable matter from the eternal. He must be able to filter all information, and retain only the good a the noble in his mind. A cool, clear head is a necessary attribute of a powerful leader.

The trunk coming down the forehead of the elephant is an instrument which can bulldoze a massive oak tree; equally, it can perform the subtle task of picking up a needle from a haystack. A capable leader must be aware of the grossest aspects of a job as well as its minute, meticulous details. Like the elephant's trunk, the discriminative faculty of a leader with an evolved intellect can help solve gross problems as well as settle subtle issues. Good and evil are represented by the two tusks of the elephant. A strong leader must discriminate between right and wrong and all other dualities, and then form his judgment before taking action.

Ganesha has a wide mouth and a large belly, indicative of a healthy appetite and enthusiasm for life. Similarly, a successful leader is ready to stomach all types of experience, whether auspicious or inauspicious. The mouse is a tiny fidgety creature that darts from one food to another, nibbling a little from everywhere. This denotes a mind full of desires, ever-hovering from one longing to another. There is a mouse within each of us, capable of eating away all merits. The mouse is surrounded by an assortment of enticing sweets but it looks up at Ganesha, seeking His permission to eat. A competent leader must check all temptations, and rise above selfish desires, personal ambitions and aspire to work for the welfare and happiness of all his followers.

Vighneshwara has four arms representing the four inner equipment, *antahkaran*. In one hand, he has a rope and in another an axe. With the axe he severs the attachments of his devotees and with the rope he pulls them closer to the Truth, and ultimately binds them to the highest goal. In his third hand, he holds a riceball (*modak*) representing the rewards of the joys of devotion to God. With his fourth hand he blesses all his disciples and protects them from all obstacles.

# A Karmayogi Who Lived the Gita

## Anil Ambani

 uly 6 will always be an emotional day for the entire Ambani family. It is my father Dhirubhai Ambani's Nirvan Divas. Many knew him as a visionary who created a business empire and became a legend in his own lifetime. But few are aware of the spiritual underpinning to his material achievements. I once asked him, "Do you read the *Gita*?" He replied, "I live the *Gita*."

In the *Gita,* Parthasarathi tells Arjuna, "No one has attained his goal without action if even I were to cease working, the world would perish. How much more necessary then for the people at large to engage in action?"

My father, a god-fearing and family loving man, who believed in karma and its effect, took Lord Krishna's wisdom to heart as a valuable lesson. But the fruits of his labour — success for his corporation and wealth for the nation — never changed his value system. He used to say, "Whatever you do, be down to earth, be humble and be simple. Humility in success is the best virtue to have."

He never wanted anything for himself. When I asked him what he missed not having, he would reply, 'education'. He wanted to study, but did not have the resources. He made up for that more than adequately by ensuring that my brother, two sisters and I got the best education. Yet, I feel that with his education in the school of life, and insatiable thirst for knowledge, he was always two steps ahead of all of us.

He was the simplest of men. He dressed in a white shirt, navy blue trousers, black belt, black shoes, and blue socks. His everyday wardrobe contained six such sets. That was enough for my father.

He didn't revel in fame. What he revelled in, was doing things. On every achievement, whether major or minor, he would be jubilant. He would take a deep breath, smile with satisfaction, and say, "Growth is life." He would be overjoyed that Reliance's 33 lakh shareholders had something more to be happy about, and that more wealth had been created, making India a stronger country.

And then, just so none of us got the wrong idea about achievement, he would reiterate — as he did so often: "Our dreams have to be bigger, our ambitions higher, our commitment deeper, and our efforts greater. This is my dream for India."

On July 6, 2002, his personal physician, Dr Pandey, told me, "Sir is a person who will not inconvenience anybody. If he goes, it will be on Saturday night, after the day's work. The funeral will be on Sunday. It will be over by evening, and on Monday morning, everyone can get back to work."

My father passed away at 11.50pm on Saturday night. The funeral was on Sunday. On Monday morning, we were all back in office. My father, who believed work is worship, would not have wanted it any other way.

I came home at 2.30am the night my father passed away. I woke up at 5am and went to tell my mother. She saw my face, folded her hands and asked, "Did he go peacefully?"

I said, "Yes, he had a big smile."

Seeing my grief, she told me, "Your father has gone to heaven — that is his permanent home. God sent him to earth on a mission. He chose India, and he chose this family. Now there are others to carry on his mission here, so God needs him back in heaven to do His work."

It was a mother's way of comforting her son. She also did it to convey the message that her husband would want life to go on.

# Just Pole-vault Through Life

## TGL Iyer

ergie Bubka, world champion pole-vaulter said, "No athlete can jump that great height without a pole. At the same time, he cannot jump that height with the pole. If the vaulter clings to the pole he will dislodge the barrier. The pole has to be discarded when he reaches that height. Only then, he can cross over and go to the other side."

Similarly, you cannot reach Godhead by clinging on to this world. You can reach it only by discarding your luggage and vaulting over to the other side. The *Bhagavad Gita* in Chapter XII, Verse 7 says, "These Arjuna, I speedily deliver from the ocean of birth and death, their mind being fixed on me." It means that God speedily exempts from birth and death, once for all, and brings face to face with Himself in this very life, those devotees who constantly worship Him. As a boatman takes his boat across the river, so does God warding off all difficulties and dangers confronting the devotee takes him across the terrible ocean of worldly existence to his supreme abode. This is what it means, reaching the Godhead."

During his wanderings in Judea, Jesus was approached by a man who knelt before him and asked him, "Good Master, what should I do to inherit eternal life?" Jesus reprimanded him for calling him good saying that none except God deserved that epithet. He asked the man to follow the ten commandments. He said, "One thing thou lackest; go thy way, sell whatever you hast, and give to the poor; and thou shalt have treasure in Heaven; and can take up the cross and follow me." The Gospel (Mark x 21-22) says further, "And he was sad at that saying and went away grieved; for he had great possessions." Seeing him thus going away Jesus made the much-quoted statement that it was easier for a camel to pass through the eye of a needle than for a rich man to enter into the kingdom of God.

Detachment does not mean severance from the world, abstinence from possession and enjoyment. It does not mean going to the forest and doing *tapas*. Great men of renunciation are found to possess and enjoy sense objects as freely as any other person. For example, King Janaka ruled a kingdom of his own. Yet Vedanta was his life-blood. Justice, compassion, sacrifice were the cornerstones of his success as a ruler.

Detachment cannot be defined by material boundaries. Lord Krishna is described in scriptures as having associated with thousands of women. Yet, he is known as *nitya brahmachari* or perpetual celibate. Sage Durvasa is associated with the consumption of large quantities of food. Yet, he is known as *nitya upavasi* — one who fasts perpetually. These are not apparent contradictions to detachment. It only drives home the truth that possession and enjoyment have nothing to do with detachment or renunciation. When does one attain a state of detachment? When the selfish ego is got rid of. It can be interpreted this way. All worldly cares, duties and responsibilities belong to the little self. When you remain detached from the world, you are free and happy. Detachment merely means casting aside your vain, accumulative and possessive spirit.

George Washington, Mahatma Gandhi, Abraham Lincoln were all great successes in their own lives. The secret of their success was that they kept themselves practically above all attachment. Undisturbed by worldly worries and anxieties, their minds were focused on something high. Their energies revolved around a specific goal beyond all selfish, self-aggrandizing and egoistic living. But the funny part is that they were not aware of their renunciation. They stumbled upon it, encashed it and brought wonderful results.

Self-development, writers always say, "Men who control themselves usually lead from the front, no matter what the mission." Two men were travelling together. They were childhood friends. One became a millionaire and the other a *sanyasi*. They reached the bank of a river and it was late in the evening. They were standing near a forest infested with wild animals. The only boatman refused to ferry them as the weather was bad. The rich man offered the boatman a large sum of money. Having reached the other side the rich friend said, "Of what use is your detachment? If I didn't have the money we would have been eaten by the wild animals?" The *sanyasi* said, "Reflect a little deeper, my friend. Was it its retention or rejection that really saved our lives?"

# The Light at the End of the Tunnel

## TGL Iyer

s a child Alexander Dumas was walking along the road when he saw pieces of a broken mirror. He picked up the largest piece and started playing with it. He discovered that he could reflect light into caves, tunnels and dark crevices where light could not enter. It occurred to him that the best way to refine the human mind is to reflect light to make it bright. With this insight, he started writing books to help uplift the human mind to reach heights — all through its own efforts.

The *Bhagavad Gita* says that nobody from outside can save us; we have to save ourselves, "Raise yourself by yourself. Do not let yourself down. For, you are your own friend; you are your own enemy" (Chapter VI, verse 5). We often tend to place the blame on others or on external factors for our failures.

Every individual has to experience some amount of fortune and misfortune in his or her life. Sometimes what we perceive as misfortune turns out to be for the good. The *Gita* further says that the self is the friend of the self for him who has conquered himself by the self, but to the unconquered self, this self stands in the position of the enemy like the external foe.

Whenever we speak of religion, we tend to recall images which are obscurantist ideas: like the sacred thread and *vibhuti* or casteism and untouchability. Sri Ramakrishna and his disciple Swami Vivekananda tried to teach religious precepts that were based on reality rather than on symbols and rituals. Their intent was to communicate a profound message of total human development, that could uncover the divine spark available within all of us.

In his lecture on Vedanta and its application to human life Swami Vivekananda says, "Bring light to the poor; and bring more light to the rich, for they require it more than the poor. Bring light to the ignorant, and bring more light to the educated, for the vanities of education of our time are tremendous."

In the *Mahabharata* Sanjaya the king, defeated in the battle-field, returns to his palace where he is confronted by his mother Vidula at the palace gate. She says,"It is better to flash forth once in your lifetime than smoke away for ages." Sanjaya went back to the battle-field chastened and inspired by his mother's words and went on to gain victory.

Jesus Christ delivered the famous Sermon on the Mount to his disciples. The sermon, however, continues to provide spiritual nourishment to millions of people even today. "Blessed are the poor in spirit; for theirs is the kingdom of heaven," said Jesus. He meant not only the external world; he extended it further to include the kingdom within us, too. The message that spiritual realization can be had here and now, in this very life and not after death, was revolutionary. Jesus said, "Blessed are the pure at heart; for they shall see God."

The Buddha said, "These two extremes, O Bhikkus, are not to be approached by him who has withdrawn from this world. Which two? That which is linked and connected with lust through sensuous pleasures and the other connected with self-mortification and pain. Avoiding both these extremes, *madhyama pratipada* or the middle road brings insight,  knowledge, tranquillity, enlightenment and peace. The middle road is the eightfold path of right outlook, right will, right speech, right action, right livelihood, right effort, right mindfulness, and right absorption that leads to peace. When the self has no consciousness and it becomes one with the Lord, you can call it enlightenment, awareness, realization and freedom from bondage."

Sage Yagnavalkya tells his wife Maitreyi, in the Brhadaranyaka Upanishad, "As a lump of salt dropped into water dissolves in water and no one is able to pick it up, but whensoever one takes it, it tastes salty, even so, my dear, this great and endless, infinite reality is nothing but pure intelligence. Because, when there is duality, as it were, then one smells, one sees, one speaks, one thinks and one knows. But when merged with the Brahman, all becomes one."

Enlightenment, it seems, is that conquest proceeding from the *tamas* to the *rajas* to the *sattva* stage when you see everything as one and separateness is obliterated.

# Eternal Values & Seven Immortals

Girish Bhandari

n the Indian tradition there are seven immortals: Aswathama, Bali, Vyas, Hanuman, Vibhisana, Kripacharya and Parashuram. They symbolize certain higher ideals. Aswathama, the son of Guru Dronacharya, was a mighty warrior. He had even learnt the art of invoking the Brahmastra, the ultimate weapon of destruction. One day, after the Mahabharata war was over, and when the Pandavas were away, he and a posse of men entered the camp of the Pandavas by stealth and killed all the male members in complete disregard of the prevailing ethics of warfare. He was later overpowered and arrested by the Pandavas.

His life was spared but his crown jewel — a gem — was prised out of his head. He was condemned to live for ever, the wound festering, never to heal. It was a warning to future generations that a great warrior's life, bereft of good conduct, is a life given to eternal suffering. That is karmic retribution. Ashwathama's flawed immortality is a grim reminder of the consequences of unethical behaviour.

King Bali is immortalized because even Vishnu had to humble himself as Vamana to conquer him. He stands out for his valour and charity — two great eternal qualities. Bali knew fully well who Vamana was. Yet, he prepared to surrender all he had, to his Lord. So this man of grace is still revered.

Vyas, the great scholar and writer, the author of *Mahabharata* and the Srimad Bhagavatam, is another immortal, a shining beacon of erudition and wisdom. A *katha-wachak* reading from the holy texts, is said to ascend the Vyaspeeth — blessed by the immortal Vyas. He comes to represent the continuity of erudition, scholarship and the apotheosis of the writer as the ultimate visionary.

Hanuman exemplifies selflessness, courage, devotion, energy, strength and righteous conduct. He stands for the potential that is inherent in all of us. He also represents the air, the atmosphere and thus the life-breath — the *prana*. Sita is believed to have bestowed on him the boon which made Hanuman ever-youthful, energetic and immortal.

Vibhisana had unshakable faith in what he believed. He was a fearless counsellor of righteousness even when all around him were given to sycophancy and peer pressure. As a follower of right conduct, Vibhisana survived unscathed while tragedy befell the unrighteous king and his followers.

Kripacharya was an extraordinary teacher. To him, all pupils were equal. A guru like Dronacharya favoured Arjuna and sacrificed an equally if not more promising student — he asked Ekalavya for his right thumb. Kripacharya, on the other hand, upheld the highest standards expected of a teacher: He was impartial.

Parashuram was master of martial arts. No one could beat him — whether the tools were *astras, sastras* or divine weapons. He had no temporal ambition. Had he so wished, he would have been the greatest Chakravarti Samrat India had ever known. But he lived a hermit's life. He was also one who never hesitated to admit a mistake. During Sita's *swayamvar*, after Ram had broken the divine bow of Shiva, Parashuram asked both Ram and Lakshman for forgiveness. Despite his excellent qualifications, he did not hesitate to apologize in all humility that he had lost his reason in anger. Parashuram symbolizes excellence and strength, tempered by humility.

These seven immortals exemplify certain basic truths, laws and standards of ethical behaviour which transcend time, locale and generation. They are universal and immutable. Their immortality is therefore not mere deathlessness — it is more the immortalizing of each divine principle they stood for and upheld even in the face of adversity and pressure.

# Bapu's Corporate Code of Conduct

## KS Ram

ll religions are unanimous in denouncing the amassing of wealth. The Bible declares: Easier indeed it is for a camel to pass through the eye of a needle than for a rich man to enter heaven. 'Wealth undoes a man' — *artham unartham*, said Adi Sankaracharya.

Fakiri, voluntary poverty, is a way of life highly commended by the Sufi saints. *Aparigraha*, non-possession, is a value emphasized by the *Bhagavad Gita*.

Mahatma Gandhi understood that it was futile to strive for a world order which eliminates commerce altogether. He knew also that business and industry cannot be conducted without involving ownership of property.

Gandhi was equally concerned about social justice. Even today there are millions of households where parents have to send their children to sleep on empty or half-fed bellies. Gandhi believed that there never is any 'absolute' shortage of food. God creates food for all; and it is the unjust, man-made patterns of possession that have created social inequality. He said, "Nature provides for mankind's need, not for his greed."

Socialists came up with a solution: Forcefully dispossess the rich and distribute their wealth among the poor. Such a solution, based on violence, could never be acceptable to Gandhi for whom means were as important as ends. He felt that any good wrought through violence cannot be stable.

The opening verse of the Isa Upanishad provided Gandhi with the first breakthrough: *Tyakten bhunjita* — 'renounce and enjoy!' Don't cling to your wealth. Possess wealth, but don't be possessive towards your possessions. Narrow-minded possessiveness leads to fear of many sorts. Fear turns enjoyment sour. In time, your riches become the very cause for your sorrow and moral misery. In respect of trade and industry, how can one renounce and enjoy?

Can one simply let go of all that one has raised through years of hard work and labour? Should one simply abdicate the seat of power and move to the woods? Supposing you do so, will not someone else grab your position, create chaos and possibly jeopardize the livelihood of all who may be employed in your industry?

Gandhi's doctrine of trusteeship does not propose abdication. He only seeks an attitudinal change in the captains of commerce."

"Not all of your wealth belongs to you; it belongs to the community: understand this," says Gandhi. Give up the binding thought of proprietorship. Transform your position of ownership into that of a managing trustee. This will give rise to a 'disinterested commitment'. This is not the same as dilution of interest; to have a 'disinterested commitment' only implies a transmutation of self-interest into corporate interest; of selfish concern into social concern. You continue to retain stewardship over the business you have raised — but for serving also the larger social interest. You become a leader in the truest sense. Gandhi believed that when the doctrine of trusteeship begins to be practiced, philanthropy as a separate activity will become redundant.

Under the doctrine of trusteeship does the managing director of a concern earn the same as, say, his peon? No. Gandhi does not propose a flat form of equality. His principle is: From each according to his calibre; to each according to his true need.

He, therefore, emphasizes equity rather than equality. Regarding succession, Gandhi is in favour of a member of the family succeeding the managing trustee, but he stipulates that this must be subject to the employees accepting the successor; else the new trustee must come to office through election.

# Is Greatness not Born of an Inspired Heart?

Debashis Chatterjee

sat breathless by the seashore in Cartagena, Colombia, on the Caribbean Coast. The air was filled with the voices of tourists and the puttering of an occasional vehicle. The sun bathed in a sensuous glow the house of the great writer, Gabriel Garcia Marquez. It was a brick-red palace presiding over the magical sea. This for me was a pilgrimage to greatness.

I wasn't only thinking of Garcia and his *One Hundred Years of Solitude*. I was thinking if one could really become great even when one had no fame or power or just a few pesos in his pocket. Is greatness not born of an inspired heart? What has greatness got to do with the world's approval? Can we not all become great even if we hadn't won the Nobel Prize like Garcia did?

A tourist guide began to describe how Marquez's friendship with Fidel Castro of Cuba had earned the anger of many of his countrymen. He pointed towards the house where Marquez and his friends spent time. He shared with me how Cartagena de Indias had been an important port on the Caribbean since it was founded. Before he could inflict any more history lessons on me, I pressed into his palm a bunch of pesos to tell him off. He declined to take the money and made a theatrical bow and thanked me with an unforgettable and exquisite courtesy. I stood humbled by his greatness!

A woman shared a table with me in a seaside cafe. Her name was Claudia. She was seeking counsel on how to mend her broken life. She stretched her finger on the table. On her right index finger was a precious green emerald. Colombia, I learnt produced 60 per cent of the emeralds of the world.

The Incas and Aztecs of South America — where the best emeralds are still found today — regarded the emerald as a holy gemstone.

"The green of the emerald is the colour of life and of springtime, which comes round in eternal cycles," I said. Claudia spoke haltingly, "But it has also, for centuries, been the colour of constant love. In ancient Rome, green was the colour of Venus, the goddess of beauty and love."

Claudia and I walked towards the sea. A divorced mother of two children, she had said, with her eyes fixed on restless waves: "My life is a waste; I haven't gone anywhere really." The sea rolled in and rolled away again.

"We come to this world alone," sighed Claudia, "and will go back alone." Not quite, I said, for we are born as one and go back as one. We are one with the world, with the vast solitude of the sea and the mountain; one with the wine flowing from the vineyard and inside our veins; we are one with light inside the emeralds and all the rhythms of the universe.

We are born of the great One — the unity of life that courses through our lives — and we will long for the One and merge with the One that is reflected in the seeming multitude of life forms. "Listen, Claudia, that infinite Oneness is the only secret and the source of all greatness!" You are not alone Claudia, you are in the company of your own greatness!

*Muchas gracias* — thank you very much — Claudia gushed as we concluded our conversation. I blurted out *de nada* — you're welcome, don't mention it. It was just about all the Spanish I had picked up from a tourist phrasebook in Cartagena.

# Receiving & Giving
# with an Open Mind

Discourse: Nimishananda Guru

o bring in a sense of purpose and improve the quality of our lives we need to look at the nature and working of our mind. The mind is meant to absorb information, transform it into knowledge and lead us to action. Action and speech determine the quality of our life and these come from the mind.

What's the nature of absorption of the mind? Seers have said that most people's minds are as hard as rock. Just as rock is impervious to water, information that falls on a hard mind bounces off without leaving any trace.

A hard mind offers resistance to information and it prevents the flow of knowledge and action. The mind that is as soft and pliable as a sponge would have the capacity for maximum absorption. Just as water can be easily absorbed by the sponge and squeezed out, a soft mind easily absorbs information and allows the creation of knowledge and action.

However, a soft or open mind can be hardened and a hard or closed mind can be softened. Hence the need to be alert.

What makes the mind hard or closed? It is said that this is an automatic, front-line defence mechanism for the protection of belief systems based on the state of ego.

If we encounter an idea or a situation that is not in line with our thinking, we immediately close our mind by blocking it. This is called mindset. Ego creates mindset. Mindset is a protective self-defence mechanism because we are scared of what others think, about our notions and beliefs. Mindset is self-destructive. A simple discussion could therefore develop into an argument and lead to conflict.

It is therefore reasonable to conclude that the mere gathering of information is useless. We must transform this to knowledge. The mind must be receptive to be able to perform this conversion efficiently. A closed mind does not allow for progress whereas an open mind would.

How to purify and soften the mind? A pure, soft mind could help us access the Divine life. Thinking positive isn't enough, thinking Divine is essential. Raising ourselves from the level of human thinking to Divine thinking can soften and purify the mind. For this we should review the working of our mind at least three times a day. Was my mind aggressive or calm? Did my words and actions hurt or bring joy to people? Because an object that slips out of our hand can be recovered, but an inappropriate word uttered cannot be retracted.

Self-review will cleanse the mind of all mental dirt. Ideas and inspiration flow freely in a pure mind to transform information to knowledge to use for the welfare of many in the form of an action. There are three basic steps that wise men have recommended to achieve this: 1) Allow others the freedom to be as they are, without imposing your thoughts and ideas. 2) Have faith and belief that God is in you. 3) Spend some time quietly everyday thinking about your Inner Self and chanting the name of God. This way the mind can help us transform our lives from the mundane to the Divine.

# T'ai Chi is Effective in Sharpening Concentration

### Sensei Sandeep Desai

oncentration is necessary for advancement in any form of creative endeavour. When the thought process becomes disjointed, the end result falls short of our expectations. To be able to truly concentrate even as long as one minute takes a fair amount of perseverance. However, with persistence and self-discipline, concentration can become natural and effortless and you can retain the awareness of one or multiple thoughts in your mind without feeling as though you are being pulled in different directions.

The untrained mind, because of its short attention span, keeps galloping in all directions without conscious control. Why do many people find it so difficult to concentrate? One possible reason is that we, in our effort to use time efficiently, take on more than one thing at a time.

As a result, we may get diverted. We tend to veer from one task to another, completely different task. The end result of our jumping from one task to another is that we don't accomplish as much as we would have if we had given our complete attention to one thing.

On the other hand, it is possible that we may get a valuable idea in the process. The purpose of concentration is not to become fixated with one thought or become rigid in our outlook. The purpose of concentration is to help us make creative use of the mind.

At each point, we must retain an awareness that we are drifting from our original task and evaluate whether this shifting is a good idea. If it is, then we should go ahead. If not, then we should revert to the task at hand. Far from being a fixation, concentration involves a higher degree of flexibility that makes the thought process smooth rather than scattered.

The practice of T'ai Chi is good for developing concentration. T'ai Chi movements help you to become aware of the extremely subtle tensions that exist between your spinal cord, internal organs and brain. Mental relaxation brought on by the slow and gentle movements helps your mind to settle, freeing it from the thoughts of the past and the future. For when the mind is relatively empty, we are more present, centred, open and sensitive.

Additionally, the movements of T'ai Chi are intricate enough to fully occupy your mind. Whether you are doing a form that takes one hour or one that takes five minutes, you are expected to do the movements without physical stops and starts — without wavering or losing concentration from whatever you are focusing on during each movement.

However, this can only be done efficiently if you are truly able to relax your mind and let go of anything extraneous to the task at hand. This increases mental stamina and also trains your mind to cultivate the same relaxed, but alert, quality at work. Being able to think with clarity and not have your thoughts jangle your nervous system allows you to focus on whatever you are doing.

Many of us tend to suffer from shrinking attention spans, possibly on account of a stressed out lifestyle that exerts undue pressure on us. Or it could be that with so many activities and distractions, we tend to get bored easily. Whatever the reason for lack of concentration, T'ai Chi could help focus your energy on the task at hand.

# Pack A Punch with Spiritual Energy

Swami Veda Bharati

e often hear phrases like 'power yoga', 'power breathing' and perhaps even 'power meditation'. These phrases convey images of a heavy punch delivered by a wrestler or a country beefing up its armed forces. However, this is not the kind of power a practitioner of meditation pursues.

The Upanishads do state that *atman* is not to be found by one devoid of *bala* or power. Here, power refers to spiritual energy. The yoga sutras of Patanjali mention *virya* as one of the five ways of attaining *samadhi* and *brahmacharya* or practice of celibacy confers *virya*. However, this *virya* arises out of *shraddha* or reverent conviction and is synonymous with the power to grant *diksha* or initiation which means *shakti-pata*, the power to transfer a higher state of consciousness to the disciple. This is the true meaning of power yoga.

The power in yoga means the power to extinguish one's anger like that of taming a wild tiger, for instance. It means the will to overcome temptation and thereby altering the mental state of one who may approach a yogi with passionate thought. It is the power of Buddha whereby he converts Angulimala, the dreaded robber who cut off his victims' fingers and wore them as a necklace round his neck. The Buddha walks into the robber's lair and says "Come along, monk!" and helps transform the marauder into a monk instantly. The latter follows him like a tiger that has been tamed. That is true power.

The power of yoga is that of *ahimsa* whereby one abandons in all possible manner, at all times, towards all beings, any inclination to hurt or harm. With that power one may approach two combating armies, stand between them and through sheer power of presence, make them lay down their arms. Alexander had massacred many in battle during his conquests. Yet, he gave up violence after meeting with monks who advocated *ahimsa*.

Chengiz Khan established a large empire by sheer force of

violence. When he reached what is now called Afghanistan, he began to have doubts; he questioned the meaning of his life. He invited a Taoist master to talk to him. The Taoist master's spiritual guidance convinced Chengiz Khan to stop his conquests and instead, set about consolidating what he had, peacefully. There is a painting depicting this in a Taoist temple in Beijing.

While the energy received from meditation may help one to win a long race, a true yogi uses the power to sit. Sitting still requires greater *shakti* or power than does running. True power is the power to stabilize yourself.

In the yoga sutras certain meditative practices are termed *sthiti-nibandhana*, establishing stability. *Abhyasa* or spiritual practice involves stable posture and undiluted relaxed concentration. During *abhyasa* your breath becomes calmer, deeper and lighter. Coupled with *manasa japa* or mental chanting, there is an even flow.

The even-flowing mind-stream generates awakening of *kundalini* whereby one may conquer all intangible worlds and states within oneself. For a self-conqueror of the interior worlds the external conquests are mere pursuit of mirages, a wastage of power. He puts a stop to this. This *virama* or ceasing is true power. We need to attain to this power of purity.

# Practice Makes Perfect:
# It Means Hard Work

Acharya Mahaprajna

hat kind of *sadhana* is it that does not result in the abatement of all passion? The whole system of spirituality and all religious tales are designed to subdue passion.

According to Mahavira, eating is the greatest obstacle to self-control; it gives rise to indolence. How can he who is not moderate in eating, ever conquer sloth? How can a person who does not get rid of lethargy, indolence and negligence, ever achieve self-control?

Begin the practice of self-control with fasting. Eat less. This is the first principle of self-control. The second relates to the body. It is necessary for us to exercise control over the body, to train it.

Start by contemplating upon and practising good habits, and by inhibiting bad habits. Our nerves and muscles are accustomed to function in a particular way and if we do not effect a change, we go on mechanically as before. We have a longing for sweets on certain occasions, because the tongue is accustomed to a particular taste. The nerves and muscles come to demand something, which they are accustomed to having on a particular occasion.

In the matter of eating, thinking or doing any other work, our sinews habitually function in the manner we have accustomed them to function. Those who live in a lofty building, are at first extremely careful while descending the stairs. Gradually, they become accustomed to the act and after some time they do it mechanically.

To begin with, the novice typists look at each letter before they type it, but with practice, their fingers move freely without the necessity of looking at the keyboard since the fingers have grown accustomed to it. Similarly, in any undertaking, our sinews start working in the manner we have accustomed them to function, and the task stands fulfilled without any conscious effort on our part.

One practises meditation today, gives the sinews a taste of

64

meditation and accustoms them to it. Next day, however, he does no meditation, nor the day after. On the fourth day, he sits down to meditate again. Practising by fits and starts does not help in the cultivation of habit. Do not be remiss. Keep practising daily. Irregular practice is not conducive to the confirmation of the habit of retrospection.

You practise forgiveness today, show tolerance, but quarrel and fight the next day, forgive again and yet again quarrel and fight — this will not confirm in you the habit of forgiveness. If you want to cultivate a habit, do it without any reservation, without any remissness till it is firmly established. That is the second principle of body training, of accustoming the body to bear pain and discomfort. This state of indifference is achieved through the practice of *asanas, pranayama* and *kayotsarga*. The body is so trained as to perform any task you command.

The third principle of self-control is living in seclusion. It means not to allow the present moment to continue but to reverse it. There are two orders — the order of nature and the order of *sadhana*. All our sexual impulses originate from the centre of energy and it is with the help of this centre that man fulfils his sexual desire. It is a centre provided by nature for gratification of sexual urge. By living in seclusion, we can change it.

# Look East Policy to Experience The Light

## Janina Gomes

eep looking to the east till the sun rises again. Those who look to the west will never see the sun rise. Similarly, we habitually look at and preoccupy ourselves with the negative. We all flee God in countless ways. We flee him along the labyrinthian paths of our own mind. We choose the path of least resistance. We seek easy accolades and flowers. We like to dwell in gracious fields where everything seems to flow with the even tide. How easy it is to be one of a crowd, to move and follow the direction they all seem to take.

Yet God seems to point another way, the path not frequently trod. There, one might often walk in darkness. Few would like to accompany us on such a path. There are few lamp posts along the way. The sun may be enveloped by fog. We may have to peer through the darkness to catch the shafts of light that strain in.

Darkness is personal, it is also social. It sets off a chain of hate-filled living that stirs up the unnatural. It pits people against each other. It uproots giant trees set up by culture and civilization. Like a relentless roadroller, it crushes what is beneath. That is what it means metaphorically, when we say look west.

Another chain operates, driven by the power and grace of God. The light it radiates is another kind of light. It is light that heals, patches up differences, protects the innocent, it creates new communities and recreates the earth. Like the child learning to walk, we learn to step out in faith. God holds out an inviting hand. He steadies us when we stumble. He throws a veil of protection around us when we are hedged and hemmed in by the darkness. The master weaver weaves, creating patterns that we are slow to see and understand.

When we look towards the east we see the first signs of the earth rising to a new day. We breathe in the salmon and pink streaks that light the sky and the freshness of the morning. The whole of creation which seemed to be hurtling relentlessly to an early death comes alive. We know deep down that we are loved and protected. The nights are no longer heralds of darkness. They are a prelude to light.

Looking east calls for hope. Hope that someday things will change. We will not be like herded cattle that sometimes stampede each other. We will trust once again. We will welcome what is yet to be born — a world not shaped by hatred and revenge, but of true human solidarity that deep down we all long for.

Perhaps we have forgotten that creation was meant to be about sisterhood and brotherhood, about loving and caring. New life born from the old is always fresh and gentle to the touch. We can catch it not only in the warmth of an infant's eyes, the shaking hands of the infirm, the mellow quietness of the old who are content with life, but also in the movement of people and nations walking towards a better life, the noise of traffic, the hustle and bustle of the city, the slow working of a village life.

Those who make the effort to look east — instead of following the crowd — find the struggle was worth the trouble taken. A new day begins. The sun rises once again. Creation turns around. For those who have no master, the flowers are attraction enough. Those for whom God is all in all, the darkness is only a prelude to the dawn. Keep looking to the east till the sun rises again.

# What Makes You a Leader is Complete Awareness

## Discourse: Shri Shri Nimishananda

oday, no one is functioning with full potential. That is why we are anonymous. Usually, one notices three patterns in the lives of people. Some lead, others follow, while many quit.

Leaders are those who have self-motivation, zeal and dedication. They have the ability to tune in to their inner Self, so they can guide and motivate others. Those who follow must have the enthusiasm to comprehend and implement the mission and vision placed before them. They must also work at transforming their own shortcomings. We see many quitters around us. They have plenty of complaints and grievances; they rarely enjoy life. They flow with worldly currents and lead mechanical lives.

What quality prevents life from becoming mechanical? What ingredient ignites zeal and keeps boredom at bay? Awareness. If we are constantly aware, life is always interesting. We enjoy everything for everything inspires us. Awareness is not alertness. Alertness requires effort and has an element of stress and tension. Awareness is alertness without tension. When we are in this relaxed state, zeal and interest are spontaneous. From interest come memory and dedication. We should do nothing mechanically. Even stirring a spoon of sugar into a cup of tea should be done with complete awareness. Then there is always a deep sense of joy and connectivity with Divinity.

We should be aware of what we are doing every second. You may feel that this will produce tension. No. We are always aware of our name and family. Does this make us tense? Awareness is a relaxed and expansive state that eliminates tension. If we are constantly aware, we give cravings no scope to take root. Even drinking a cup of tea can be done with complete awareness so that we savour every sip. Then the tea is enjoyed by the body, senses and mind. There is satisfaction and no craving.

When we fulfil a desire mechanically, the deeper levels of our being are not satisfied and we develop an obsessive craving for that object. Lack of awareness also generates indifference for others, while awareness creates complete connectivity with Divinity and all beings. Without this connectivity we are not open to divine grace though it is flowing to us constantly. When we are conscious of connectivity, we live in a state of heightened awareness.

We often strive to amass property for future generations. Physical property may be lost. It may lead to strife and litigation. The best legacy we can leave behind is awareness and wisdom. *Mahatmas* are remembered with reverence not for the property they amassed, but for the principles by which they lived.

The outer world is constantly changing. The cars that are today's status symbols will be the bane of tomorrow. All material things lose their value after a while. Divinity never changes. God is ever the same. Divinity transcends time and space. Awareness of Divinity takes us to the only state that is worthwhile — constant bliss that is independent of bodily existence.

When we stop imposing conditions on life, we surrender to the divine tempo. Then our life becomes a feast of bliss. We embrace life with open arms. We become natural leaders who inspire and ignite the flame of awareness in every heart.

# Let's be Enthusiastic about Life & Living

Discourse: Swami Sukhabodhananda

tudy the life story of successful people and you'll find that they have tremendous enthusiasm or passion to live life. Edmund Hillary who was the first to reach the summit of Mount Everest with Tenzing Norgay, had failed thrice earlier. Later at a party hosted in his honour in New Zealand, he looked at the portrait of Mount Everest and said, "Mount Everest has a problem. The problem is, it cannot grow more than about 29,000 feet, whereas I have the ability to grow in my ability to climb Everest."

Every one of us has a lower self called *jeevatma* and a higher self called *paramatma*. When you operate from the lower self you find your life is not powerful unlike when you function from the higher self. This is the choice before us.

Living from the lower self makes life threatening. Living from the higher self makes you enthusiastic and opens up opportunities. Any situation viewed as a threat is an example of something that involves the lower self. The lower self operates as an interfering or obstructing thought whereas the higher self operates as a supporting thought.

If your body's immune system is weak, your system is vulnerable to disease. Similarly, if your psychological immune system is weak you get upset, hurt, frustrated. Like our genes, our minds are also products of evolution of many years. When our psychological immune system is weak, we are prone to perceive external situations as dangerous or as obstructions. It only calls for strengthening the psychological immune system so as to be powerful individuals.

How do you make your mind powerful? We strengthen the physical body with exercise and diet. The psychological immune system can be made powerful by not allowing the lower self in us to operate, instead we should encourage the higher centre to operate in our daily lives.

Where do we draw our identity from? Mostly from acquired knowledge because that's how ego, identity and address are established. Ego is established in the 'I'. Acquired knowledge is the lower self. The knowledge from which we are born — the cell evolution — is the higher self.

Acquired knowledge should support the higher self, not obstruct it. For example, in a game of tennis, when you see a ball coming from an opponent, your thought should not interfere with it and obstruct your spontaneous effort to hit a ball. But if you think, "Oh, I am going to miss it because I missed a stroke last time," then acquired knowledge is obstructive. As a player, you cannot succeed.

The higher self would look at the ball in a different way — "With a focused awareness I allow my being that has evolved to guide me in hitting a ball. In case I miss it, the higher self being a learning and evolving being, makes required corrections the next time I face a ball whereas the acquired or lower self creates an image that I am not good and I am not lucky. This image makes me look at a ball next time as a threat and acts as an obstruction. The lower self is rigid, while the higher self is flexible in learning and growing."

So say to yourself, "I will not allow my static conclusions to decide my action. Instead, I will allow my flow to decide a response."

# Prayer, Faith & Doctors Could Make You Well Again

Robert Klitzman

will pray for you," a senior psychiatrist told my patient. His comment surprised me. I was in training, and the patient was a petite Latina woman who had remained despondent despite medication, psychotherapy or anything else I did. Would he really pray for her?

Occasionally, as a trainee, you would spot a hospital chaplain but at medical school, nothing about religion or spirituality is ever taught. Science is supposed to be logical, rational and objective, while spiritual beliefs are irrational, subjective, elusive and hard to describe. Not surprisingly, research suggests that doctors tend to be less religious than their patients.

I began to look at these issues differently after my sister died in the September 11 World Trade Center attacks, leaving me stunned and depressed. I was now a patient. As I recovered I began to wonder about other doctors who had become patients I ended up interviewing more than fifty of them. I soon learned that when doctors get sick with serious disease, they also tend to reconsider their spiritual beliefs

I spoke with doctors and several said they were religious before they became patients, but they were admittedly even more so once they faced serious illness. Others changed more dramatically. "Patients used to ask me to pray for them, and I'd pooh-pooh it," one elderly physician told me. After he got sick, he 'realized how important prayer was'.

Often these doctors expressed a hodgepodge of beliefs, drawing on the organized religion in which they were raised, and adding elements of eastern philosophy or New Age beliefs.

That said, some physicians weren't changed by illness, remaining sceptical and disillusioned with organized religion. "I see it helps my patients," one doctor told me. "I wish I had it in my life more. But

I don't." It could not always be willed.

Some doctors felt that prayer can directly alter the physical process of healing through God's intervention. My view is that prayer and faith give vital strength and motivation that can help patients cope and continue to fight.

Does it matter whether you and your doctor share the same spiritual beliefs? I would argue that your doctor's personal beliefs don't matter. What matters is that your doctor recognizes that your beliefs are important to you. Training cannot convince doctors to become more spiritual. But it can, I hope make them more aware of the range of views that their patients have. Religion is a huge area that many doctors don't know much about, yet this is what our patients are thinking about. I hadn't appreciated the extent of that, until I myself became a patient.

Thinking back to the senior psychiatrist who told my patient he would pray for her, I now realize how astute he was. I saw her as a little, depressed woman. What he picked up on was that Catholicism would be important to her. That was the way to connect with this woman who so far had rejected our efforts to help her. At the time, to me, it seemed an odd thing to say. In retrospect, it was quite empathic.

As an intern, alas, I was usually too busy to discuss these issues with patients — not yet aware of their significance. But I hope now that future doctors will do better. It will help patients. And their doctors too.

# A Teacher's Tribute to Her Dear Students

Chitra Srinivas

eaching is my passion, and luckily my experience as a teacher has been beautiful, emotional and fulfilling. Over the years, I've watched the student-teacher equation evolve: From guru as God, guru as all-knowing — *"Guru Brahma, Guru Vishnu, Guru Devo Maheshwara, Guru sakshat, Param Brahmn tas mai Shri Guru vai namaha"* — to guru as friend and equal, as someone who doesn't always know best.

Today's guru and *shishya* are partners in the process of teaching and learning. We inspire, motivate and learn from each other; if I don't know, I can admit it to my students. The teacher is only a facilitator, one who will help the student grow to her potential, become a self-learner. The teacher is only one of many sources. Not infrequently, there is a role reversal. With children being so tech-savvy, often I am the student and they are my teachers.

Has teaching changed the way I think? Yes, most certainly. My students have shown me how to manage time. I marvel at how deftly they juggle sports, academics, dance, theatre and pottery, for instance. I have learnt how to accept failure as I see my students taking success and failure with equanimity. I admire the confidence of my students who can go up on stage and speak extempore. I see them contesting an election, lose it, and yet work with the winner for the common good.

I have observed students working in teams, giving suggestions, disagreeing politely, coming to a consensus even if it means giving up one's original idea. They go ahead, never claiming, 'That was my idea'. I see them sharing everything — their history notes and lab coats, their problems and joys, their ice creams and food, with such ease. It is wonderful the way they appreciate their classmates' talents. If you ask them "Who do you think should be given this task?" you can be sure they will pick the most suitable person. Their

74

loyalty to friends disconcerts me at times. Will their selflessness last as they grow into adults?

Students are so good at solving problems creatively. The other day as I was walking out of the school gate, I saw something interesting. One girl, recently elected senior-most student leader, was motivating her fellow students with an amusing game — to amazing response. When I questioned her she told me it was an activity to energize them so that they could put in their best for the forthcoming Teacher's Day function. How innovative!

My students have often shown me how to keep cool during a crisis, with a "Don't worry ma'am, it can be done!" I am often amazed at their openness, at their ability to think critically, accept reasoned answers. What has struck me most is their daring — to chart unknown territories, to be constantly redefining rules, unafraid to be original.

My students make me think constantly. Last week I told my class, "In these 10 years of teaching from this book, no one has asked me this question!" I have to be always ready for surprises. I know they are not testing me — though they do, sometimes. They ask such basic questions that it stumps me.

I have taken so many things for granted. Students remind me that my learning is not complete and never will be. Above all, my students have taught me to be young, to never grow old. I have to be up-to-date in everything, in order to keep up with them.

# Getting Inspired by Anyone, Even Yourself

### RM Lala

hile inspiration can come to anyone at any time, you can create a conducive climate within you so that you get self-inspired. For self-inspiration, both your heart and mind need to be relaxed, so that you are in leisure mode.

Isaac Newton was relaxing in the garden when he saw an apple fall. He had the leisure to ask himself why the apple fell straight on the ground and did not go upward. He found the answer and propounded the law of gravity.

Sometimes small incidents can result in the creation of a major work of art or literature. Edward Gibbon's *The Decline and Fall of the Roman Empire* is an acclaimed work in the English language. In his autobiography he writes that when he was in Rome he sat musing amidst the ruins of the old city. Barefooted friars were singing vespers or evening prayers. This is when he got the idea of writing about the decline and fall of the city. The realization of this idea took many years but his persistence and hard work resulted in a classic of literature and not only of history.

Galileo was sitting in a church when he saw a chandelier gently moving from side to side. He noted that the to and fro movement of the chandelier — that was independent of the bob mass or the amplitude of the swing — would prove useful as pendulum for keeping time like the metronome that aids students of music.

Many of us live under the tyranny of the next thing to do on our list. Sometimes leisure is enforced on us as during convalescence. A temporary immobilization from routine activity suddenly creates the time for self-evaluation. For a writer or teacher a sabbatical provides the leisure for him to think through a subject.

Leisure by itself is not enough. It has to be accompanied by mindfulness and attentiveness. Sometimes inquisitiveness is an aid to inspiration. The second aid to inspiration is concern for others.

Many of the medical inventions have come from a desire to cure a disease.

Inspiration has to be followed through to yield any result. Thomas Alva Edison said, "Genius is one per cent inspiration and 99 per cent perspiration." For want of application and follow-up, many an inspired thought is lost. Our quality of life shapes our inspiration. An uncluttered mind is likely to be receptive to even small whispers from within.

Nature is a wonderful source of inspiration. I remember a time when I was depressed after a course of chemotherapy and was sitting in the garden when a *mynah* gave a full-throated cry of joy. She repeated the cry again, twice and I could not help but experience her joy as my spirits lifted.

Music is soothing; it also inspires. What comes out of us depends on what goes into us. It is worth asking from time to time: "What is my intellectual and spiritual input this day? Who are the people I think of apart from myself ? Who are the people I can help?" Inspiration comes from reaching out.

For our rushed lives the prayer of the American poet, John Greenleaf Whittier, is so relevant:

> Drop thy still dews of quietness,
> Till all our strivings cease;
> Take from our souls the strain and stress,
> and let our ordered lives confess,
> The beauty of Thy peace.

# Laughing & Learning
# the Traditional Way

Chakyar Rajan

ndic epics are replete with stories of the interplay of divine incarnations, human beings and animals. The characters and events in these works serve as guides for social conduct. Infused with Vedic wisdom, these narratives are easily understood even by those who are not aspirants for pure Vedic scholarship. The large number of Puranic episodes containing multiple characters led to the growth of visual presentations on stage like dramas, ballets and dance forms like Kathakali, Bharatanatyam, Kuchipudi, Manipuri and Yakshagana.

All this led to the evolution of folk art with regional variations that command vast audience participation. Folk art characters — heroes, demons or genies — are portrayed by artists with elaborate and colourful make-up.

Humour was an important aspect. Specific humorous characters like the *vidushaka* or royal clown came into being. *Vidushakas* conveyed a lot of wisdom in their apparently idiotic sayings or gestures. In fact, they not only act as fools; they make the audience laugh and think at the same time. A circus clown who attempts grotesque acrobatics and tumbles down often in the ring or trapeze with a scream is always a highly accomplished performer.

In Kerala, as in some other regions, Sanskrit theatre underwent a transformation, thanks to the encouragement of the then rulers, the Perumals. In the dance-drama Subhadra Dhanamjayam, three principal characters — Arjuna, Subhadra and the Vidushaka — were portrayed on stage, in theatres called Koothambalams located mostly in large temples. Naganandam is another such drama. The dance-drama that developed in Kerala was called Koodiyatam, which means dancing together. Since characters in Koodiyatam spoke in Sanskrit, the *vidushaka* conversed in the local vernacular Malayalam so that most of the audience could understand. Whatever the *vidushaka* said or did would provoke hearty laughter during the Koodiyatam performance.

To address a wider audience unfamiliar with Sanskrit, an offshoot from Koodiyatam popularly known as Chakyar Koothu came into existence. The characters for Chakyar Koothu are *vidushakas* who are solo performers. With the minimum of Sanskrit prose and poetry the *vidushaka* expands each word to weave the story fabric in Malayalam, which is understood by every one in the audience. In his narrations, which are often dramatic and exaggerated, the aim is to bring out the inherent absurdities in human nature. The idea is the listeners will naturally correct themselves if they have such weakness or deficiencies in them. It is like making you learn after you've had a good laugh — metaphorically, sweetening a bitter pill.

Dry presentation of spiritual values may not be easily assimilated and may often appear boring to the listener and hence the recourse to humour and mirth. Humour makes life more interesting and livable. Today, we have laughter clubs all over. The writer has attended several assemblies where spiritually eminent personalities have spoken and even though the audience sits peacefully and silently, the intensity of the interest is often missing. The meetings are more like ceremonial ritual.

Spiritualism, whether it is Vedantic, or yogic or devotional, can be better imbibed with a dose of humour free of the profane or obscene. One need not act serious or appear glum while immersed in a serious subject like spiritualism. Gravity and humour are not antipathetic to each other. They can, and they should, coexist, so that one cannot only learn to laugh but learn while laughing.

# Energy-giving Sun as a Symbol of Pure Love

Soma Chakravarty

n the physical realm, the sun is the centre of illumination in the solar system. In the spiritual realm, the sun is perceived as the intermediary of God's will. The sun as life source is an incessant flow of essential love energy, enlightening our consciousness, revealing that we are part of supreme consciousness.

All beings are imbued with a spark of clear inner divine light, the light of our real nature, say Buddhists. The holy Qur'an describes man as a candle flame burning in a niche in the wall of God's abode. Allusion to light as a symbol of a formless God can be found is most faiths. This is the light that radiates everywhere within and without. *Jyotiaham,* the splendour in the Self.

The spiritual journey is inevitably a quest for this divine light that takes us through the subconscious and self-conscious to superconsciousness. From darkness to light, to enlightenment. The Yoga Sutra of Patanjali says, "The heart and mind can find peace and harmony by contemplating the transcendental nature of the true self as supreme effulgent light."

Swami Surya Jowel, practitioner-teacher of Surya Yoga explains that just as the sun makes every thing visible, this form of yoga gives us light to see our innermost self. When you look at the sun the radiant rays of light enter the self, completely purifying; removing mental, physical and spiritual obscurations. When we meditate on the sun — as our inner *surya* on the *ajna chakra* or 'third eye', the door of wisdom — it destroys *maya*, the dualist concept or illusion and takes us to the state of glorious emptiness, which is the real nature of existence.

When we receive the pure energy of sunlight, it cleanses our spirit and fills us with the pure spiritual energy of love. Desires flow through us like ceaseless waves of oceans. Surya Mudra, which consists of interlinking of fingers of the right and left hand, help to control our senses; it is the symbolic merger of male and female principles. Desires of the personal self are transmitted into love of the whole. When we do *suryayog* with *surya mudra* we obtain freedom from the claims and demands of the physical, emotional and mental domains.

In this context the sun becomes our *sakha* or guide, helping us get attuned to deeper and deeper comprehension of true nature of Brahmn, the absolute, the *atman*, our true self. The energy of the sun expands our limits and opens us up to imbibe wisdom, compassion and sublime consciousness to feel the pulse of pure energy or love.

"Pierce the darkness and you will come to that which is not shrouded in darkness, pierce that again and you will see it as it were a wheel of sparks, throbbing with the colour of the sun, mighty and vigorous. Brahmn beyond darkness, shining in the sun and in the moon and lighting. Seeing Him, you will become immortal," says the Maitri Upanishad.

Hence the sun, symbolically, is reality which is beyond divisions. Once you turn to the sun to experience the effulgence of inner energy, union with the universal soul becomes possible. When energy is perceived as love that is all embracing, positive thoughts take over and peace prevails.

# True Charity Helps You as it's Unconditional

Yogi Ashwini

harity is the most important tool for spiritual evolution. You'll know why if you do this simple test: Stand up and start inhaling. Go on inhaling. To ensure that no breath is given back to the atmosphere you must go on inhaling. Do not exhale. But no matter how strong your lungs are, you will have to exhale at some point. It is impossible to hold on to your breath endlessly. Do you realize that even something as precious as life-giving breath cannot be hoarded? For it would result in destruction.

One of the five *yamas* in the eightfold path of yoga translates as charity, a purification. We all think charity is giving something to the needy. What we give away is not ours because you are only the channel. But charity is 'done' and not given. You only do something for someone without expecting anything in return for it. The left hand should not know what the right hand is doing because it is not the right hand's business to know.

A person who makes an exhibition of his charity is not doing charity; he is merely buying fame. The world's resources belong to everyone. Someone gets a bigger share someone gets a smaller share, but these resources are meant for each one of us. So, if you are bestowed with fortune, blessings and the capacity to share, then you should just give, without any doubts or questions in your mind as to what use it will be put to, without thinking whether this person is worthy of it or not. There should not be any judgment attached to that act. You should not worry about what you gave to someone, or the use it will be put to. That is not your business.

In the *Bhagvad Gita*, Krishna says, "Judgment lies only in my hands," what lies in our hands is the karma, the action. In order to judge another human, you ought to be perfect first and we know that only the Divine is perfect and no one else. When you judge means that your state of mind is interfering with the charity you are doing, then you are merely doing it for personal satisfaction. Charity should be free of judgments and attachments. Just thinking that one has done a good act by giving something to someone indicates his attachment with that act. If you feel good, happy, satisfied at the end of any action that means that action was done for your own self. Charity should be done and forgotten.

Charity need not be expressed in money. Charity can be kind words; it can be helping someone; teaching or blessing someone, it can even be something as simple as a smile if someone needs that, at that moment, without expecting anything in return. It can be any act of help to someone without being directly benefited by it. Your work is only to act and do your karma as a channel and not count your blessings. For instance, Indra came to Karna to ask for his armour and Karna knew that it was Lord Indra and why he was asking for the armour. Yet, since Indra came with both his hands spread out, asking, Karna just gave it. That is charity.

# An Extraordinary Dinner that Changed My Life

## Shaily Mishra

ne night God appeared in my dream and asked me to have dinner with Him the following night. The venue was the restaurant not far from my home and the time was 8pm. I was confused. Should I go ahead and keep my dinner appointment with God or dismiss the invitation as a crazy dream?

I was haunted by the dream the whole day. The dream was vivid and I knew I would regret it all my life if I did not go. I did not tell anyone about it for fear of ridicule. I would be the laughing stock of the family. This will have to remain a secret. By 8pm I was already seated at a corner table in the restaurant where God had said he would meet me for dinner.

All my five senses were on high alert — I didn't want to miss even the slightest clue of God's presence. My ears were eager to hear the sound of a slight movement of chair, my eyes wanted to see the chair moving back a little and again taking position with no one appearing to move it. After all, God is invisible! But He would definitely give me some indication of His presence. Maybe He'd whisper into my ear! Finally the chair moved, but to my disappointment it was my uncle — who I hadn"t met in a long time — who plonked himself on the chair.

"Are you waiting for someone?" he asked.

"No," I replied quickly.

"I'm alone, too, so let's have dinner together," he said. I nodded uncertainly. "How about some chicken curry and rice?"

I looked around but saw no sign of God. Where could He be? Maybe I was taking my dream far too seriously.

"Er... I won't eat non-vegetarian food," I replied.

"Great, so when did you give up nonveg?" asked uncle.

"Actually, I haven't given it up, it's just that I don't want to eat it tonight," I said.

Uncle said, "But if you think it's wrong, you shouldn't have it at all. Why turn vegetarian on a particlar day? OK. We'll have vegetable curry."

Dinner was over. God did not appear. It was uncle who spoiled my dream. I was upset. When I went home, I blurted to my parents the story of my dream and the dinner with uncle.

Dad said, "It's good to see God in your dreams. Dreams do come true. It's only we who refuse to see the dream coming true as it happened in your case. You have been waiting for God with all your five senses alert. But to feel the presence of God, you need to invoke your sixth sense. If only you'd used your sixth sense, you would've realized that you did in fact have dinner with God — only, He appeared in the form of your uncle." I laughed at the idea. Then what was His message to me?

"Well," said Dad. "He did give you a message. Didn't he say that if you thought that something was wrong, you should avoid it all days rather than only on specific days?" So, does God want me to turn vegetarian? I asked. "No, God said if you think it's good, you can have it on any day. For God all days are same, all months are holy."

Dad went on to explain to me that religions are created by us, human beings, with dos and don'ts. However, it is more important to have an honest (personal) relationship with God. So it is better to treat God equally on all days of the week and all months of the year.

85

# Enlightened Communication is a Creative Process

### Andrew Cohen

ost people don't know how to communicate. We share information, sometimes in very sophisticated ways, but we don't really communicate. Real communication is a creative process. Human beings evolve only through interaction, so enlightened communication means engaging in a developmental process at the highest level of our own consciousness, literally creating a new edge of evolutionary potential through the act of communication itself.

Enlightened communication can occur in a disciplined, controlled context, where the content of the dialogue is kept in the realm of the impersonal. If you hold yourself and other participants to the biggest philosophical and spiritual concepts, without swerving into abstractions or deviating into personal matters, you will discover that the liberating depth and clarity of the Authentic Self will spontaneously emerge. You'll find yourself unusually awake, oblivious to the passing of time, because your conversation occurs in a context that is infused with ecstasy and evolutionary tension.

The instant you or anyone else become too abstract or personal, this new context that you have created together in consciousness will disappear, the evolutionary tension will dissipate, and you'll lose touch with the Authentic Self. But if you diligently avoid mere opinions, theoretical abstractions, and the personal dimension altogether, your words will become one with the inspired passion, focused intensity, and evolutionary tension that emanates from the Authentic Self. And once you become grounded in the Authentic Self, eventually you will be clear enough to be able to slowly widen the content of the dialogue to embrace all of your humanity, including every aspect of the personal domain, without ever swerving from a truly enlightened perspective.

Enlightened Communication is communication beyond ego. Once

the ego is out and the Authentic Self is released, all participants find access to a kind of knowing and cognitive capacity that has nothing to do with any prior accumulated knowledge. They find access to the source of wisdom itself.

Traditionally enlightenment has been an inner revelation, an expansion of consciousness and a higher state of being that an individual would discover within herself. But now we find that as we evolve, our spiritual capacities are also evolving and it's possible to find access to enlightened consciousness beyond the internal subjective experience of the individual.

When this higher state emerges between us, what was once a subjective experience becomes an inter-subjective experience. Because we meet in the Authentic Self, the difference between one and many disappears and the enlightened mind becomes one voice speaking to itself. In this profoundly awakened context a truly revolutionary potential is revealed. It's a window into a completely new order of human relationship in which we not only awaken to this higher level of consciousness together but, even more importantly, begin to engage with it in order to find out how to create the future.

# Don't Give in to Stress, Just Learn to Manage it

## Umesh Sharma

tress levels of students are on the rise, pressurized as they are to perform superlatively in examinations. Stress is also the bane of executives who are dogged by competition and ambition. Stress-related ailments are becoming more common. Stress is different things to different people. To a mountaineer, it is the challenge of pushing physical resources to the limit by striving to achieve a demanding goal. To the motorist, it can be the hassles of heavy traffic and pollution.

Stress is a major problem for many, but curiously, it is also a matter of pride in certain circles. The perception is that if you are not stressed, you are just not working hard enough. You toss and turn all night. The alarm doesn't go off. You're late for work. There's a deadline to meet, but your computer is down with virus. Three cups of coffee later, your head still throbs. Your back hurts. Your eyes sting each time you blink.

Stress is the inability to cope with a real or imagined threat to your mental, physical, emotional and spiritual well-being which results in a series of physiological responses and adaptations. It can be caused by both good and bad experiences. The Upanishads say that we are a part of the world and the world is a part of us. As human beings, we live at several levels. Coping refers to our efforts to manage stressful situations.

Make a list of possible sources of stress; it will help you understand and pay attention to issues that are a source of stress. We might have a classic case of 'stress overlap' when everything seems to be going wrong, all at the same time. Be aware. Take a moment to determine your main source of stress at the current time and work towards managing it.

People are often reluctant to reveal that they are stressed and will resist any suggestion that action needs to be taken. As such stress sits in the 'shadows', hidden from view. This will continue until it bursts out into the open by which time it might be either too late for remedial action or damage control becomes costly. A further shadow can be seen when an executive chooses not to intervene in a potentially difficult situation where someone appears to be stressed. This might be because he doesn't know how to deal with it and so feels embarrassed at exposing his lack of knowledge. Alternately, he might take a 'let sleeping dogs lie' approach and just hope that it will go away. Either way, the stress situation gets worse and recedes deeper into the shadows and thus becomes harder and costlier to address at a later date. Everyone responds differently to stress. That is why some people seem to thrive during stressful situations while others are exhausted. Pressure is inevitable. The solution lies in active management. Pressure is a neutral force; it can be channelled for good or bad. Pressure can be the stimuli we need to enjoy our lives and learn new skills, experience excitement and get things done. It can also be the force that causes depression and anxiety, miss deadlines, break relationships and even become seriously ill.

Resilient people accept responsibility for their life and their choices, and they understand what's gone wrong and then try to fix it. So they are able to cope with stress. Those who are not naturally resilient can learn from the examples of others.

# The Spirit of Adventure
# is Essential in Life

Discourse: Swami Sukhabodhananda

e need to balance both security and insecurity. I have
seen people who always look for insecurity and risk.
They are uncomfortable with security. I also find some of
them being imbalanced.

The spirit of adventure has to be included in your life. Truth has
to be searched for. In a search nothing is guaranteed. The only thing
that is guaranteed is a beautiful adventure that helps you grow. In
such an adventure, you learn the art of both accepting and rejecting.
Then you would be able to filter many things in life.

Do not get lost in adventure. Rather, find yourself in adventure. If
you are getting burnt-out, then something in you asks you to slow
down. There is a God in us who speaks, but our mind is noisy and
thus we cannot hear the divine speaking. When you are inwardly
silent and addictive thoughts are absent, the silence and the
meditative energies that emerge will heal you.

Then, walking is meditation, sitting is meditation, and drinking
tea is meditation. Most often, the burnt-out feeling is from your
thoughts, which signal that you are burnt-out. Bring a meditative
quality in your thoughts. Watch out not to use words which are self-
defeating. Bring in the quality of joy in whatever you do. Allow your
actions to flow from the 'higher self'. The 'higher self' guides you
when to slow down.

Learn the art of relaxation. After a long run, sit under a tree, feel
the miracle of your body, the dance of your breath, the music of your
heart beat, the gentle kiss of the breeze... the quintessence is in being
relaxed, being at ease with oneself. Whatever you do, let your centre
be calm, silent and relaxed. Act from this energy field. Let action
emerge from silence. The nature of your 'higher self' is silence,
peace... while that of the 'lower self' is restlessness and ambition.

Flower gives fragrance unconditionally, so let us also operate from unconditional love. All great masters inspire us to live in abundance but not in scarcity. Be total and not fragmented. Live to the maximum and not to the minimum. Let your 'presence' reach others and shower them with fullness.

Real growth happens when you trust and operate from the 'higher self'. This 'higher self' is a flow, a learning being that enjoys the given moment in totality. Unfortunately, we trust our 'lower self' that is authoritative, rigid, and non-supportive. It is a victim of likes and dislikes. Growth happens when you negate the 'lower self' and are centred in the 'higher self'. Your 'higher self' is an evolving being through which you come in touch with a mystic flower in you.

A courageous person explores the unknown with or without fear or in spite of fear, whereas a non-courageous person is stopped by fear. Respect what you know and have courage to explore the unknown. The courage of a spiritual seeker is different from the courage of a soldier. The spiritual seeker drops his mind and explores the heart... it is a flight from the head to the heart... has courage to accept even death as he knows the art of living involves the art of dying. By accepting death, he has accepted life in totality.

To accept both life and death gracefully requires courage. Failure is a shadow of the ego. With this understanding, life becomes magical. The hidden secrets of life flow in us. One cannot succeed against the whole. One's success is the success of the whole. In fact, one becomes the whole.

'You are the fullness. There is fullness, here is fullness. From the fullness, the fullness is born. Remove the fullness from the fullness and the fullness alone remains,' say the Vedas.

# You can Take Charge of Your Life

## Discourse: Sadhguru

 henever things don't happen the way you want them to, there is a temptation to name it destiny. This is how you deal with failure; you are consoling yourself. Whatever situations you are living in, to be human means that you can mould situations the way you want them. But today, most people in the world are moulded by the situations in which they exist. That is simply because they exist in reaction to the situations they are placed in. So their question will be, "Why was I placed in such a situation? Is it my bad luck, is it my destiny?"

Everything that you know now as 'myself' is just an accumulation. Your body is just an accumulation of food. What you call 'my mind' is an accumulation of impressions that you have gathered through the five senses. What you accumulate can be yours; it can never be you. What is you is yet to come into your experience; it is in an unconscious state. You are not even hundred per cent conscious of what you have accumulated. You are trying to live your life through what you have gathered, not through who you are.

You have acquired certain tendencies depending upon the type of impressions you have gathered. This can be changed. Irrespective of your current tendencies, your past experience of life, your genetics, irrespective of who your parents were, where you were born, where you grew up, if you do certain things with yourself, you can change this. You can completely rewire yourself in 24 hours' time.

A century ago, many things that people believed to be destiny or God's will, like diseases, infections and death are today in our hands because we have taken charge of certain things. What we call technology today is just this: Within the laws of nature, everything on the outside that can be taken charge of, we will take charge of someday.

As there is an outer technology, there is an inner technology or inner engineering. Everything that this life is, is naturally happening to a certain law. If you know what the nature of life

92

within you is, you can completely take charge of the way it happens. Then would you let any unpleasantness happen to you?

Unpleasantness is happening to you in the form of anger, fear, anxiety and stress because your basic faculties — your body, mind, emotions and your life energies — are doing their own thing as if they don't belong to you.

It doesn't matter who you are. Life doesn't work for you unless you do the right things. Existence is not judgmental. Good, bad, all these judgments are essentially human and socially conditioned. Every society has its own idea of what is good and bad, but existence is treating all of us the same way. Whoever is receptive right now gets the bounty of life. The whole aspect of yoga is to make you receptive.

If your experience of life transcends the limitations of the physical, you become available to Grace. Suddenly you function like magic. Other people may think you are magic but you know you are just beginning to become receptive to a different dimension of life. And for everybody, this possibility is wide open. When it comes to outside realities, all of us are differently capable. What you can do, somebody else cannot do; what someone else can do, you cannot do. But when it comes to inner possibilities, every human being is equally capable. You are not any less capable than a Buddha or a Jesus or anybody for that matter. All of us have the same inner capabilities, unfortunately never explored, never accessed.

# C'mon, Together Let's Inspire the Youth

K Rama Prasad

Dear Senior Citizens,

Those of you with more than sixty years of experience in life have been part of or have witnessed the many ups and downs of the journey. Some of you have had a good life, commendable up to this point, and some of you have struggled to reach this stage. But all of us, I'm sure, agree that whenever we were successful, our confidence level was very high. We have realized that success is directly related to confidence. Some of us acquired confidence from encouragement and guidance from our elders while some others have not been so fortunate. Some of us struggled in life and learnt through experience after many failures. Now at this stage, we are all having a lot of valuable experience and the maturity to analyse our lives and find reasons for our failures.

After entering the senior citizens' club, our responsibilities have increased in many ways. Maybe, we need no longer have to go to a working place to earn a living as we might have opted to learn to live with our savings. But it is our spiritual duty to guide the youth for a better tomorrow. In introspection, we can see that we would have been more successful had we received guidance at some stages of our lives. Peace, happiness and self-confidence are essential forces for a spiritual life. We might have missed these life-enhancing forces due to lack of guidance and proper advice whenever we were in adverse situations. Guidance in teenage years is as fertilizer to growing crops. All of us have learnt a lot from our mistakes. In addition to that we have learnt from history and scriptures to make us wise and ripe enough to impart our experiences to youth for their growth in the right direction.

Today's children are more fortunate than we in terms of information access but they also get lots of negative information along with positive inputs. So our role is more specific, to guide them to right information for a peaceful and happy life. Advice to follow truthful path with honest and sincere efforts and to cultivate virtuous mannerisms can be given to youth of today to help them become achievers.

Terrorist activities, misuse of power, scams in every walk of life and health problems like AIDS due to ignorance are common. The youth today are often subject to negative environment and then their self-confidence is affected adversely. Stress at educational institutes and work-places are creating restlessness in their minds due to which they are all struggling in their lives despite good education and decent family backgrounds. As senior persons, we can bring back peace and happiness in the minds of struggling youth by speaking to them and advising them as to how to set their goals in this competitive world without being under stress all the time.

Seniors should talk to youngsters frequently, explaining the various benefits in achieving a goal by sincere effort and hard work where they get maximum happiness in their accomplishments. Such frequent and regular friendly interaction with them would be beneficial as our suggestions would at some point reach their subconsciousness and maybe get acted upon. Youngsters could spend some time in meditation to keep their body and mind healthy. Serene waves from minds of youth interact with the turbulent minds of those who often contribute to setbacks. So, let's guide the youth to cultivate a positive attitude and to put in sincere efforts with self-confidence, so that the young of today can learn from the mistakes of the older generation.

A Senior Citizen

# Everything You Wish
# To Know About Success

Discourse: Swami Nikhilananda Saraswati

uccess can be measured from two standpoints — the external and the internal. Externally it is the measure of a job well done and recognition. Internally it is a feeling of achievement and wholeness derived from the completion of a task or the fulfilment of a desire. Is a true measure of success the outer accolades or the inner joy and peace that is experienced when we know we have performed well?

Our goals are based on our desires and aspirations. When we fulfil a desire or achieve a goal we feel happy and successful. But shortly another desire arises and we feel incomplete and begin to strive again. Occasionally, when we reach a goal we feel a void in our lives and do not know what to do next.

Success can also be measured by the feeling of comfort we have with ourselves. This happens when we live according to our intrinsic nature. If we attain what we want and still find something lacking then we know that either our desire was not desirable or the means adopted were not in accordance with Nature.

Modern management philosophy says that if a person is satisfied there is a lack of motivation and this works against the interest of the corporation. This is a negative approach. When people are positively satisfied, they want to share their feelings with others. Their motivational levels get higher. They want to work more and also efficiently.

Swami Chinmayananda, founder of Chinmaya Mission, went all over the world, reaching out to people not because he desired anything. He did it out of a joy of sharing what he had, so that others may benefit and partake of his knowledge, good fortune and success. It was an expression of the joy he felt within. True success is that which gives happiness to self and others.

Success should include and embrace all aspects of life. Some may be great at work but utter failures in the family arena. Some may be good in the family but are of no use to society. We must be whole individuals, just as God intended us to be. Take the case of a mango seed that grows to be a tree giving the world its sweet fruit. The seed does precisely nothing, but by remaining true to its nature finds fulfilment and completeness.

After returning from Lanka Rama was asked how he won the battle. Rather than taking the entire credit he acknowledged the contribution of all those who had helped him. Giving credit to the whole team is the hallmark of a great and true leader. When Hanuman returned from Lanka after locating Sita, he did not go directly to Rama to give him the news. He collected all the other monkeys and included them in the successful completion of their mission.

Why do people want success? It is associated with perfection, wholeness and joy. It is an expression of our Higher Self which is Supreme and perfect. We have this thirst for success because we are that Supreme alone. We want to be great because we are intrinsically great! It is a natural desire fulfilling its natural goal. If we understand this in all its connotations then our success will not be dependent on anyone's failure, nor will it be gained by pulling others down. Our joy will emanate from a deep sense of contentment and completeness.

# A Picture in My Wallet after all Those Years

Babujee Datta

 ticket collector in a train found an old worn out wallet in a compartment full of people. He looked inside to find the name of its owner. There was no clue. All that there was in it was some money and a picture of Krishna. He held it up and asked, "Who does this wallet belong to?"

An old man said, "That's my wallet, Sir, please give it to me." The ticket collector said, "You'll have to prove that it is yours. Only then I can hand it over to you." The old man, with a toothless smile said, "It has a picture of Krishna in it."

The ticket collector said, "That is no proof; anyone can have a picture of Krishna in his wallet. What is special about that? Why is your picture not there in it like most normal people?"

The old man took a deep breath and said, "Let me tell you why my picture is not there in it. My father gave this wallet to me when I was in school. I used to get a small sum as pocket money then. I had kept a picture of my parents in it.

"When I was a teenager I was greatly enamoured by my good looks. I removed my parent's picture and put in one of my own. I loved to see my own face and my thick black hair. Some years later, I got married. My wife was very beautiful and I loved her a lot. I replaced my picture in this wallet with a picture of her. I spent hours gazing at her pretty face. When my first child was born, my life started a new chapter. I shortened my working hours to play with my baby. I went late to work and returned home early too. Obviously, my baby's picture occupied the prized position in my wallet."

The old man's eyes brimmed with tears as he went on. "My parents passed away many years ago. Last year my wife too left her mortal coil. My son, my only son, is too busy with his family. He has no time to look after me. All that I had ever held close to my heart is now far, far away from my reach. Now I have put this picture of Krishna in my wallet. It is only now that I have realized that He is the eternal companion. He will never leave me. Alas! If only I had realized this before. If only I had loved the Lord all these years, with the same intensity as I loved my family, I would not have been so lonely today!"

The ticket collector quietly gave the wallet to the old man. When the train stopped at the next station, he went to a bookstall at the platform and asked the salesman, "Do you have any pictures of God? I need a small one to put in my wallet!"

When a man ceases to have any attachment either for the objects of senses or for actions and has renounced all thoughts of the world, he is said to have attained yoga. One should lift oneself up by one's own efforts and should not degrade oneself; for one's own self is one's friend, and one's own self is one's enemy.

He who regards well-wishers, friends, foes, neutrals, mediators, the objects of hatred, relatives, the virtuous and the sinful alike, stands supreme. The yogi, who has subdued his mind and body, and who is free from desires and bereft of possessions, living in seclusion all by himself, he should constantly engage his mind in meditation. (The *Bhagavad Gita*, Chapter VI 4-5, 9-10.)

# Krishna & the Flower
# Seller in Nathdwara

Isabelle Remitti

 ast year, I was feeling very depressed for just something unknown. It was a feeling of living a caged life without being able to do and contribute what all we desire and would like to. And then I decided to come to India for a break.

One fine day I planned to visit a temple which is quite well-known in the state of Rajasthan. It is near Udaipur and the place is called Nathdwara. The temple is known to worship a form of Lord Krishna and attracts millions of devotees especially from the state of Gujarat and other places.

I was unable to decide on my itinerary — should it include a visit to this temple? I was not very inclined to do service to God and being a foreigner didn't particularly help the cause. So I thought to buy some flowers for the deity as a small service on my part.

Since there are a multiple choices of vendors it is difficult to choose any one particular flower seller. But somehow I caught the voice of this old and poor man who was trying to sell his flowers at a very attractive rate as they were the last lot left with him.

I bought the flowers and paid him as per the rates. While returning I just went to him again and started talking to get some first-hand information. I enquired of him about his flowers and where he got them from, which he described with great enthusiasm. And so I also asked whether it will be possible for him to take me to his farm where he got these flowers. Surprisingly his answer was in the positive. We then decided to meet the very next day at 11am, by which time he would have finished selling his stock of flowers.

At the pre-appointed time I was there. After taking a 10-minute rickshaw ride we were outside the town. He then started moving through the open fields and asked me to follow him quietly. In between he used to stop at small temples where he prayed. He appeared somewhat different to me. He distributed *prasad* to the children and the poor we met on the way. He then stopped to feed the little ants on the ground.

He was walking briskly and I had to move fast to catch up with him. He then did something which amazed me. He started telling things which I used to think and ponder over. It was amazing to hear those things from a poor farmer in a remote place.

On the way back I could not resist to see the place where he fed the hungry ants. And there was lying this peacock feather which is considered as the sign of Krishna. It was not there earlier, and neither was there any peacock in the vicinity. I took the feather as a kind divine gesture.

The next day I went again to the temple to see the man. He was still there but the enthusiasm was missing. He was his normal self but didn't display any emotions towards me. I felt a little embarrassed.

I came back to my small hotel room to think over all the incidents. And then I realized it was the lord who has met me through this man to make me realize certain things. I am grateful to him for sharing a few hours with me and telling me things which were close to my heart. I knew for certain that one can meet God in the crowd or any other place. These are his ways, one just need to pick the clues and follow Him with all faith.

# Serenity Springs from Concern for Others

Muthusamy Varadarajan

he true test of one's *jnana* or supreme knowledge and awareness lies in how one greets death; the fear of death is a potent and ever-present fear. Even Dasaratha was not immune to grief and anguish, although one may say that in his case, this condition came about because of his recollection of the foul part he played in banishing Rama to the forest and agreeing to crown Bharata in his stead.

On the other hand, we have the sterling example of Bhishma who, lying mortally wounded on a bed of arrows, yet awaits with total equanimity the onset of the *uttarayana*; with death but moments away, the old patriarch finds the time to teach the Pandavas *dhana dharma, raja dharma, moksha dharma, stri dharma* and *bhagavad dharma* delineating the norms of right conduct.

In his final moments, he extols the grace of Sri Krishna towards his devotees, and passes gently into eternity. This Bhishma is able to do for he has lived by *dharma* all his life: the poet tells us that, as it slips away from the earth, his consciousness merges with the Lord. Sri Krishna himself applauds Bhishma in the words: *"Mam dyayati purusha vyagraha"* I am ensconced in him.

In our own age, Gandhiji did not curse his assassin, but died in serenity, knowing that one part of his great, self-imposed task was done; the words 'Hey Ram' emerged unbidden, almost, from his lips, the natural culmination of a lifetime of having repeated the Lord's name.

How does one arrive at this state of Supreme Consciousness? Not, certainly, only by invoking His name at the very last moment after a life of action motivated purely by selfish desire, in which the ends justified the means with no thought of right or wrong, of the victims of one's actions. The essence of *dharma* in life is to recognize the equality of all human beings, and to do what one can for their well-being all the time. Can one not, in an effort to cultivate the qualities of mercy and charity, emulate the Tamil king Pari, who, seeing a jasmine creeper wilt without support, abandoned his chariot for it?

Cannot one recall the poor lady of the house who had just one aonla fruit to enable her husband to break his fast on a *dwadashi* day, but cheerfully gave it in alms to the young *brahmachari* Adi Sankara who was promptly inspired to compose the Kanakadharastavam, whereupon, the story goes, Mahalakshmi rained golden aonlas on the lady's house?

The story has it that the goddess asked Sankara what would happen to the fruits of past karma if they were routinely obliterated thus. Sankara's answer was that the lady had demonstrated such overwhelming kindness that all her past records were wiped out by that one act of grace.

We have, in our history and our lore, a myriad other examples of such divine charity. Apart from kings and emperors, sages and saints, *alwars* and *nayanmars*, we know of ordinary men and women who exhibited such grace and concern that it earned them salvation.

Tiruvalluvar says, "*Virundhu purattada than undal sava marundheninum vendar patranru*," (If one ignores the guest and eats on one's own, even if it is nectar on one's table, it would lose its value).

This is a most practical philosophy; it certainly animated Gandhiji's practice, and today, it might be argued that it is a positive exhortation to NGO action! Gandhiji's teachings have been rapidly forgotten in this country, even though we regularly commemorate his birth and death anniversaries.

The words *swaraj* and *swabhiman* seem to have been wiped from our lexicon: we have no sense of self-worth or self-effort, and leave it to outside agencies and higher authorities to sort out problems which we should have addressed ourselves. It would be more than worth our while if we could remember just one declaration of the Mahatma's, "I shall not rest till I have wiped every tear from every eye of every poor countryman of mine." And let us do it on our own, without looking to the government to provide the support structure.

# Satsanga Changes Life & Spirit

## Seema Burman

hy do people attend *satsanga*? Are they of any real benefit? Once Buddha approached a lady for *bhiksha*, and this was the question that she posed to him. He in turn asked her to prepare buckets full of *kheer* for him the next day when he would answer her query. The next day he came back with a bowl filled up to the brim with cowdung and asked her to pour the *kheer* in it.

Dumbfounded, the lady poured buckets and buckets of *kheer*. Initially the *kheer* spilled on the earth but gradually, the cowdung spilled down with the sheer force of the *kheer* and the bowl became clean and filled up with the sweet *kheer*. A serene Buddha explained, "I have demonstrated the effect *satsanga* has on a stained soul. Constantly pour *satsanga* on the hearts and minds filled up to the brim with lust, hatred, attachment, desire, selfishness and viciousness till complete clarity and total cleansing is achieved. Only then will you be able to see your goal of achieving the Ultimate Reality clearly. Only then will the Divine Love manifest."

During 1997-99, Sant Shri Aasaramji Bapu held spiritual discourses in the jails of Patna, Ujjain and Bhopal. After the four-day discourse a prisoner in the Patna Jail confessed that the *satsanga* was his first experience of such kind and he had decided to turn a new leaf. Likewise, the story of the remarkable behavioural changes in a Norwegian prisoner Leo Sande Gasnier currently lodged in Tihar jail, serving a 10-year rigorous imprisonment sentence on charges of drug peddling, has so impressed people in his home country that the Norwegian government has decided to introduce Vipassana classes in their country's jails.

Shri Aasaramji Bapu explains, "*Satsanga* teaches you to remain poised amidst the vagaries of life. *Satsanga* is a practice where you train your mind to chant God's name, where you develop love towards God by listening to the scriptures. Spiritual development is the only thing that one carries from one birth to another. That is why you have examples of self-realization as early as in a five-year old

Dhruva, a six-year old Prahlad, an eight-month baby while still in a womb — Ashtavakra, a teenage Meera, and many more. These souls had developed love for the Ultimate Reality in their previous births and the *samskaras* showed in the forthcoming birth. Narada himself was the child of a poor widow who worked as a maidservant. Once her employer sent her to cook for a few *sadhus*. On her request they taught the child the path of devotion. Guided at an early age the child got immersed in Divine Love and became Sage Narada."

If *satsanga* erodes one's bad karmas and bad habits why don't all devotees transform? "Because," answers Bapuji, "they don't contemplate on what is being preached. It is easy to be initiated into *deeksha* and accept a Guru but how many follow what he preaches? One needs to keep a constant vigil on the mind or else it happily reverts to its old habits that have been cemented in the past births. The powerful and *saatvic* vibrations of the *satsangas* cleanse the blood cells, the nervous system, the mind and the heart. Not everyone becomes a Valmiki out of a dacoit, but some changes do take place in everyone's day-to-day behaviour. When the Guru is like Sri Ramakrishna Paramhansa and the disciple is like Narendranath remarkable changes are bound to take place. Goswami Tulsidas had proclaimed — a millionth second spent in the company of a self-realized saint erases countless bad karmas. When king Parikshit was cursed to die within seven days, saint Sukhdev advised him to listen to the discourse of Srimad Bhagwad Katha. After doing so, Parikshit was blessed with Self Realization. Even today devotees organize a seven-day Bhagwad Katha hoping for a Divine Realization."

Bhagwan Shankracharya puts a query, *"Kim durlabham?"* What is the rarest of things? And answers it, *"Satguru, Satsanga, Brahmvichar"* — Self-realized guru, spiritual discourses and thoughts of God. The threefold combination of these three is rare to find. If a man finds a *Satguru* but is unwilling to follow the preachings then he will still hanker after the worldly things. If he goes to *satsangas* but does not have the blessings of a *Satguru*, neither does he contemplate on God; he will remain engrossed in *Maya*. When a man has pure thoughts he would still need a *Satguru* and constant *Satsanga* to prevent him from falling back into his old habits. One who has all the three will surely merge with the Supreme Soul sooner or later.

# Make Time Now for Higher Pursuits

KS Ram

ost people see money as the starting point of exchange, a means to acquiring goods and services. To be able to access more and more of goods and services, we strive to acquire more and more money, working extra hours.

What we often tend to forget is that money comes at a real price. Money is not the first point of exchange in this world: it is an intermediate point. You earn money for a good life, and, ironically, even as you are struggling to earn money, you are exchanging your good life for it. Pursuit of money can become an end in itself. It can distort all values, and make you blind to the basic purpose of life.

Henry Thoreau discusses this phenomenon in his celebrated book, *Walden*. When you, for instance, build a large and grand house, or buy a new car, how do you understand the cost of your acquisition? You may express it in terms of how many rupees you have paid.

But this amount represents a certain number of years of your labour and earnings, a definite part of your life. Thoreau prefers to understand the cost of any acquisition in terms of how large a portion of life you had to expend to acquire it. If the cost of a house is the equivalent of, say, a decade of your toil and earning, the expenditure on the house is 10 years; equal to maybe 12.5 per cent of your entire life.

Thoreau's view of economy in life is how to minimize the portion time on toil devoted to organizing food, clothing and shelter, so that the bulk of the prime time is available for attending to callings of a higher value in life.

The situation in our present day world is most often the opposite of this. Most of our life is spent in the pursuit of money. Even the education of the children is chosen with the purpose of equipping them for this pursuit. Result: Occupation tends to become the sole preoccupation, until acquiring money becomes a way of life, drowning the very habit of thinking about any higher pursuit.

Thoreau sees much of what passes as livelihood as a fool's

penance. He pities young men in his town 'whose misfortune it is to have inherited large estates'.

Ego-driven, men expend the best part of their life to raise their social status in a fool's paradise. If and when they do get to it, they find it hardly fulfilling. Having made it to the top rungs, they cannot descend, because they fear a loss of face; and so they continue to pay with the balance of their life to maintain their 'position'.

A successful CEO expressed this irony in the form of a sequel to the fable of the fox and the grapes. The fox, failing to reach the grapes, 'rejected' it as sour. His friends, however, said he had failed and so he was calling the grapes sour.

The humiliated fox was provoked into action — while his friends slept, he worked hard for long hours, practising the high jump. One day, as his friends watched, he jumped and deftly grabbed the grapes. The fox earned their respect and titles were conferred upon him.

The poor fox, however, discovered to his dismay that the grapes he'd managed to attain were in fact sour. How could he reject it now? Would he not be jeered at? The fox had reached the point of no return; he must feed on, pretending to eat the sour grapes with great relish. Miserable and unable to share his secret, the fox eventually fell ill and died.

# Don't Muddy the Pure Stream of Mind

## Sudhamahi Regunathan

 teacher and his disciple were travelling, for it is said that travelling helps acquire knowledge. The journey was hot and tiring; finally they reached the edge of a lush green forest. The master said to the pupil, "Young man, we shall rest here for the night. I hear the sound of water. Will you go fetch some to quench our thirst?"

The young man hurried forth to carry out his masters bidding. On reaching the little rivulet that was gurgling past, he was happy to see that the water was clear and pure. "I'll fill it to the brim and take it to guruji," he thought to himself. So joyous was the young man that he even paused to look admiringly at a beautiful purple flower by the wayside. Suddenly, he saw a bullock cart cross the river to the other side. Carrying some wares, the cart driver was singing loudly — keeping time with the jingle of bells tied round the bullocks necks — as he drove across the shallow waters. The young disciple stood still.

The cart had unsettled the waters. The water that looked pure just a little while ago was now slushy, dirty and chaotic. How can one drink this dirty water? Disheartened, the disciple traced his way back to his master.

"Sir," said the dejected pupil to the master. "A cart just drove across the waters and the waters have become muddy. So I could not fetch any." The guru asked him to go back a little later when the waters would have settled. Half an hour later the young man picked up his jug and went to fetch water. The waters had not yet settled. For the rest of the day, he kept repeating this, thirst unquenched. The waters were still muddy. At dusk, the disciple went for the last time and returned with an empty jug.

The master smiled. "Have you learnt anything from this?" he asked the student. The disciple said, "What, noble sir, is there to learn? When a cart traverses through a stream, it brings up the slush. One has to wait for it to settle. What else is there to know?"

The master called the disciple to his side. "Sit down," he said.

"Such is the state of our minds too. If one cart crosses the river and it takes so long for it to settle down, can you imagine how many carts cross our minds and how much longer it should take to settle down? Can you stop the flow of thoughts? Purity, clarity and a tranquil state is the experience of consciousness. This is possible only when thoughts are emptied out, in a thoughtless state, when bullock carts stop traversing our minds."

Acharya Mahaprajna explains that spirituality is the path of purity of consciousness; the awakening of a consciousness that develops because of sublimation of attachment and aversion. This results in an appeased mental state and the true experience of peace and freedom from inner turmoil. For this, concentration and a strong resolve are necessary. Will power is more powerful than any bullock cart, it can stop all intrusions at the banks of the river (mind). Perhaps of greatest importance is the need to restrain emotions.

Today, most of our problems are caused by volatile emotions. They agitate our minds and make it slushy. We have to learn to exercise control over emotions through meditation; you have to watch yourself, your thoughts and your soul as distinct from the body. We have to wait patiently for the agitated mind to settle down in order to attain bliss.

# Heroes of Non-violence Show Way to Peace

## Daisaku Ikeda

aily reports of violent incidents round the world make many of us feel helpless and hopeless. We wonder how we could possibly make a difference. The thing to remember is never to lose hope, for however small the effort, every individual effort makes a definite difference.

Mahatma Gandhi expressed this very clearly: "You have to do the right thing. You may never know what results come from your action. But if you do nothing, there will be no result." Martin Luther King Jr declared: "Our lives begin to end the day we start being silent about the things that matter."

When we look at the lives of Gandhi and King, two individuals who literally changed the course of history, it is easy to think of them as superhuman. Yet they were the first to stress that every single person has a vital role to play. Gandhi said, "I have not the shadow of a doubt that any man or woman can achieve what I have, if he or she would make the same effort and cultivate the same hope and faith."

There are those who predict that the struggle of the 21st century will be between civilizations, or between religions. I disagree. I am convinced that it will be between violence and non-violence. It will be a struggle between the human impulse towards destruction and hatred and our capacity for constructive action and love. What lessons can we learn from the lives of two of its greatest practitioners, two men who led huge numbers of people to freedom and dignity?

The essential nature of non-violence is that it is rooted in the inner, personal transformation of individual human beings. As a result, the changes that are realized in society as a whole through genuine non-violence are fundamental and enduring.

Mahatma Gandhi's efforts began with such an inner change. As a boy he was painfully shy, always worried people would make fun of him. Even after passing his law exams, he remained timid. The turning point came when he was riding in a first-class carriage on a train in South Africa, and was ordered to move to the freight van. When he refused to do so, he was forced off the train. Gandhi stayed awake all night, debating on whether he should take a stand and fight for human rights.

He realized that it would be cowardly to run from his fears — so he squarely faced and challenged his timid nature, determined to confront injustice. From this inner change came one of the greatest movements of the twentieth century. Gandhi realized that human beings are the true starting point of all change. This parallels the Buddhist way of thinking. A great inner transformation — what I call 'human revolution' — in just a single individual can help achieve a change in the destiny of a nation and further, in the destiny of all humankind.

Ultimately, it was their faith in people that enabled Gandhi and King to maintain their strength under all circumstances. Unfettered by narrow nationalist or sectarian concerns, both men saw each of the world's inhabitants as fellow citizens equally lit by the inner brilliance of life. And they believed that our highest duty is to be loyal to the voice of conscience that issues forth from deep within each one of us. Both Gandhi and King each painfully experienced the overwhelming forces of violence. Yet, they never abandoned their trust in human beings.

# Principle of Samata: Unity of Being

Purushottam Mahajan

he path of spiritual progress leading to Self-realization, propagated by Gurudeva Mangatram is the Surat Shabd Yoga, the path advocated by a number of spiritual teachers like Vasisht and Patanjali in ancient times and saints like Kabir and Guru Nanak in mediaeval times.

Gurudeva's teaching includes the themes of *bhakti* yoga, *gnana* yoga, *nishkam* karma yoga and *surat shabd* yoga. At this stage of experience, the *mulmantra* was revealed unto young Mangat: Om Brahman alone is being, without shape and form, One without a second, all pervasive, blessing incarnate. To him, the Supreme Lord, we offer our salutations.

Gurudeva was born in 1903 in Rawalpindi district which is now in Pakistan. He lived a life of deep meditation, austerity and inward solitude. This twentieth century saint, through his deep insight, revived the ancient *samata* spirit of the Upanishads. His philosophy was shaped through the divine inspiration he derived from mining ancient wisdom. Gurudeva's utterances have been collected and published in two *Granths*: Shri Samata Prakasha and Shri Samata Vilas.

Gurudeva would often experience the descent of the revelation of the word. The flow of revelation would continue like the flow of water in a stream. Gurudeva said, "When divine rapture pours out, the intellect becomes inoperative — it does not think in terms of dualities. In that state of wakefulness, no wrong word can possibly be uttered. Only he who has realized the blissful state within can know what the freedom from thinking is.

When the intellect is merged into the word, right thoughts rise up spontaneously and without thought-activity, the revelatory words rush out on their own. Nothing remains concealed in that state — neither the world nor its Creator. Hidden secrets reveal themselves with absolute clarity."

Mahatma Mangatram lived a life of complete celibacy — *naishtika brahmachari* and renunciation. He devoted most of his time to the worship of God through *smaran, dhyan* and *samadhi* and in the service of the poor.

He exhorted the people to become wide-awake, to use their intelligence and power of discrimination to understand the true path of *Dharma*.

Five cardinal principles laid down by him, which can help us to achieve self-realization are: Simplicity or *sadgi*, truth or *sat* selfless service or *seva*, right association or *satsangh* and right remembrance of God or *satsmaran*.

Gurudeva said that the cessation of strife, conflict and violence will not be realized unless the sense of I-am-the-doer (*kartapana*) is not eradicated. It is the sense of I-am-the-doer that is at the root of the problem and gives rise to desires which create suffering. Also it is this "I" that gives rise to dualistic forms of thinking; the "other" is treated as an object that has to be possessed, and so has to be looked upon as something inferior. So the sense of doership should be eradicated, and it is upon its eradication that one's cosmic vision is opened up, which means there arises the vision of Unity of Being in terms of which the "other" is seen as one's own self.

Gurudeva Mangatram's teachings establish a correspondence between the macrocosm and microcosm, and thereby is affirmed the principle of *samata*, or what we call the principle of unity of Being, as the *coincidentia oppositorum*. The one who has attained *samata* has gone beyond the conflicts and contradiction of opposites.

# Follow Your Dream with Faith & Hope

Anonymous

nce there were three trees on a hill. They often discussed their hopes and dreams. The first tree said, "Someday I hope to be a treasure chest. I could be filled with gold, silver and precious gems. I could be decorated with intricate carving and everyone would see my beauty."

The second tree said, "Someday I will be a mighty ship and I will take kings and queens across the waters and sail to the corners of the world. Everyone will feel safe during the journey because of the strength of my hull."

The third tree said, "I want to grow to be the tallest and straightest tree in the forest. People will see me on top of the hill and will think how close I am to God and the heavens. I will be the greatest tree of all time and people will always remember me."

A few years later, a group of woodsmen came upon the trees. Looking at the first tree, one woodsman said, "This looks like a strong tree, I think I should be able to sell the wood to a carpenter," and he began cutting it down. The tree was happy, because he knew that the carpenter would make him into a treasure chest.

At the second tree the woodsman said, "This looks like a strong tree, I should be able to sell it to the shipyard." The second tree was happy because he knew he was on his way to becoming a mighty ship.

When the woodsmen came upon the third tree, the tree was dismayed because if they cut him down, he would never realize his dream. The woodsmen said, "I don't need anything special, so I'll take this one," and he cut it down.

From the first tree, the carpenters made a feedbox for animals which was placed in a barn and filled with hay. The second tree was used to make a small fishing boat. His dreams of being a mighty ship carrying royalty were dashed to the ground.

The third tree was cut into large pieces and stored in a dark place. Years went by and the trees forgot about their dreams. Then one day, a man and a woman came to the barn. The woman gave birth and they placed the baby on the hay in the feed box made from the first tree which they found in the manger.

The tree realized he was cradling the greatest treasure of all time. Years later, a group of men set off in the fishing boat made from the second tree. One of them was tired and fell asleep. Soon a great storm arose and the tree didn't think it was strong enough to keep the men safe. The men roused the sleeping man awake and he stood up and said 'Peace' and the storm stopped. The second tree (now a boat) knew now that he had carried the King of Kings across the waters.

Finally, someone came and got the third tree. It was carried through the streets and people mocked at the man who was carrying it. When they stopped, the man was nailed to the tree (now shaped like a cross) and was raised in the air to die at the top of a hill. The third tree came to realize that it was strong enough to stand at the top of the hill and was as close to God as was possible, because Jesus had been crucified on it.

So when things don't seem to be going your way, always know that God has a plan for you. If you place your trust in Him, He will give you great gifts.

Each of the trees got what they wanted, though not in the way they had imagined. We don't always know what God's plans are for us. Even if His ways are not our ways, they are always the best.

(From a message being circulated on the Internet)

# Gita as Guide for Today's Youth

Jaya Row

hen I say that the *Bhagavad Gita* is an ideal guidebook for the young, the reaction is almost always: "*Gita* for the young? Wasn't it meant for retired people? Who has the time to read the *Gita* when we are already under so much pressure every day of our lives?" Wait, hang on, I tell them perhaps the *Gita* can help relieve those very pressures and enable us to overcome stress and threat of failure.

Youth is characterized by boundless energy, the spirit of adventure and thirst for new horizons. Yet today the young seem bored. So many options are available to them — it is like eating different types of exotic food but without salt. All that is required is just a dash of salt to make the fare more palatable. So it is with life. The *Gita* lends taste to life like does salt to food. Just a sprinkling is enough to bring back the excitement in life, not only during our youth but right through life. So I would say that the *Gita* is an essential ingredient in life.

In this age of intellectual capital you are busy acquiring the latest skills and expertise in the belief that it will guarantee success. But success comes only when you put all that knowledge to use. For example, you need the knowledge during examinations or at a job interview. But you get so nervous that it is not available to you when you need it most. You blank out in the exam hall.

The *Gita* introduces you to your inner personality. The intellect which reasons and discriminates and the mind which is the centre of emotions and impulses. The mind is like a virus in a computer and the intellect is like anti-virus software. The former corrupts your database, the latter protects it. So only when the intellect is in command of your personality, you can access the knowledge that you have so painstakingly acquired. When the mind is playing up, the 'Access Denied' sign flashes on your screen. So alongside academic education you need to invest time and effort in developing the intellect to achieve success. So the *Gita* could be the password to success.

You must be driven not by passion but by a vision, not by the desire to arrogate but to abnegate. Go beyond mere feeding and clothing to satisfy your own deeper, more meaningful aspirations. A lofty ideal keeps the mind from devolving into chaos and poor work. The ideal is the vitamin that fuels performance. Prosperity is the collateral benefit which comes as a result of working for a nobler cause.

Physics tells us that an object is red in colour because it absorbs all other colours except red — which it reflects. Amazingly, what it gives it retains. What it takes, it loses. So it is with life.

The more you give the more you get. Dedicate yourself to a higher goal. And see the phenomenal results. What is the driving force behind your action? Is it merely prize money, personal landmarks and records? If so, you will soon get bored with life.

If you have a powerful emotional motivation you outperform your own standard and excel. Further, if you are dedicated to an intellectual ideal, you have access to far greater reserves of energy. Rise still higher to offer your talent as an act of worship to the divine power and you can make the impossible happen. Tap your potential.

So go ahead, connect with the *Gita*. Embark on a journey to transform your life from one of mediocrity to that of excellence.

# Learn to Lead from Within Yourself

## Thomas M Easley

hat defines a gathering of individuals as a religious organization? Belief? If so, why is a belief in god defined as a religion whereas a belief in free enterprise is not? Should all beliefs be defined as religious and all that is believed in, defined as God? If they do, are we free to assume that all who believe are equal in their belief and equally illuminated by the presence of 'God'?

Those who create and support a free enterprise entity do so because they believe they will benefit from that organization. Equally, believers in God maintain their belief because to do so benefits them. So there is no distinction between those who believe in a divine being, a country, family, gang, group, cult or fashion statement. The adage that 'all men are created equal' is wholly applicable when taken to mean that all men believe and all believers aspire to glorify the subject of belief. Then why do we disagree to the point of violent conflict when the subject of belief for one man differs from that of another?

We often disagree because leaders and subjects of belief are not regarded as equal in their capacity to bestow benefit upon the believer. A belief in god, for some, has more value than a belief in atheism or family, for instance. All organized bodies are similar — whether they are defined as religions, corporations, political parties, sports leagues or environmental movements — because they are created by the need for benefit. Also, they are sustained by leaders who strive to regulate social norms through manipulation of belief and the eventual control of food, water, shelter and property, the hereditary and archetypical roots of man's power.

The greater the perceived religious or spiritual value a subject of belief has, the more intense its imaginative interpretation and vulnerability to manipulation by corrupt leadership. Any belief renders the believer malleable in the hands of group leaders and equally subject to harsh reprimand if he doubts the supremacy of his group identity and his behaviour contradicts the prevailing behavioural standards dictated by the subject of belief.

Behavioural regulation is essential to an organization's vitality and its longevity. In the absence of rules and its conformity there can be no cohesive group identity, no repetitive standards upon which to attach acceptance of group morality, no means of securing loyalty and no justification for leaders to assume possession of the believer's will, his individual identity and his personal possessions.

A believer needs no proof of the existence of what is believed in. He will make no separation between himself, his belief, and the subject of belief. He will defend 'the faith', see non-believers as less pure, less moral and less right. Any challenge to his belief is a challenge to him, a direct affront to his 'God'. He becomes one with his group and perfectly programmed to defend the group.

We fight because we follow. Were all men leaders with none to follow, differences in the subject of belief would not evoke conflict as each man would feel the gain and loss of every other man. Belief in leadership would then become unnecessary.

An individual human body is a self-organizing system. There is no leader in the body, not one single cell, gene, system, or organ that leads the rest. All the body's parts work as a whole and not as parts in search of a whole. The degree to which man will evolve will be measured by man's ability to wean himself of the illusion of leadership.

# All Warmongers are Driven by Sentiment

## KM Gupta

hy are wars waged? Why are some conflicts never resolved? All fanaticism, militancy, terrorism and war are flashpoints of *ativada*. An *ativadi* is one who carries an opinion, viewpoint, argument or a case of grievance to excess. That's why sages have said: *Ati sarvatra varjayet* — Avoid excesses everywhere. No case or argument is strong enough to be an excuse for excess, for breaking peace. A mantra in the Mundaka Upanishad says, "It is one and the same life-force that shines forth as all these beings. One who realizes this never becomes an *ativadi*" (3.1.4).

The UN was established in 1945 with the express purpose of defending peace on earth. Five-and-a-half decades later, we are still living in the midst of war — peace continues to elude us.

Why have we failed to put an end to all conflict? "It is in the minds of men that wars begin, and hence it is in the minds of men that the defences of peace must be constructed," says the UNESCO constitution. So how should we go about constructing defences of peace in our minds? All militancy, terrorism and war have their matrix in sentimentalism, which is another word for *ativada*. It is this that causes wars. By reining in sentimentalism we can bring about peace.

Sentimentalism has been defined as loving a thing more than God loves it. God loves his creation; for Him to love His creation is to love Himself. But since his creation is a diversity and change and decay are its constant, He has his proportion. The sustenance of creation is God's proportion. God wants us to not love anything more than He Himself loves it; He wants us to be in tune with His proportion. When we love a thing more than God loves it, when we sentimentalize, when we take to *ativada*, we become out-of-sync with God and his proportion.

Just how much is too much? Just how much is *ativada*? When and where the thing you love ipso facto gets you to hate others, that's when your love turns into sentimentalism. We have to love our opinions, viewpoints, nationalism, religion and all that, but not to the point of making them the cause for hating others. God has no enemies in his creation. If we have, and if we see our enemies as God's enemies, that is the symptom of our 'excessive' love of our being *ativadis*.

When you sentimentalize, you are a potential fanatic, militant, terrorist or war-maker. If your *ativada* doesn't develop into full-blown terrorism or war, it is only because you didn't have the means or logistics. Analyse the rhetoric or conduct of any militant, terrorist or war-maker. Sentimentalism is the motivating force which convinces him that killing others or oneself is not too big a price for what he 'loves'. It is by sublimating sentimentalism and bringing humanity up to God's proportion/eye-view/attitude that the defence of peace can be constructed in our minds.

When Swami Vivekananda went to Kashmir he visited a shrine which had been vandalized. The sight hurt the Swami. He asked the goddess lying mutilated, in extreme anguish: "O Mother, the All-powerful, why did you allow this to happen to you and your house?" The Mother reportedly retorted: "What is it to you, my son, if my sons did this to me and my house?" The Mother, in effect, was saying, "Vivekananda, don't love my idol and my abode more than I myself love them. Don't be out of tune with my proportion. Don't be sentimental, don't be an *ativadi*. By feeding and nursing sentimentalism, even a timid, peace-loving person can be transformed into a rabid militant in search of 'revenge' and 'justice'."

# Dream Up Solutions
# with Focused Mind

Anil K Rajvanshi

n 1953 three major events took place: Mount Everest was 'conquered' by Edmund Hillary and Tensing Norgay, scientists Watson and Crick discovered the DNA's structure and a young American PhD student, Eugene Aserinsky, discovered rapid eye movement (REM) sleep. During REM sleep the brain is extremely active and generates dreams. This was the beginning of a whole new area of research in sleeping and dreaming. Fifty years later there has been tremendous progress in mountaineering and genetics but the subject of sleep and dreams continues to mystify us.

Most religions and cultures view dreams and sleep as mechanisms to connect the present physical world to that of the supernatural. Before Buddha's birth, his mother Queen Maya dreamt that a white elephant has entered her body. Similarly, Ramakrishna's mother dreamt that a small green figure, whom she identified as God, was telling her that He will be born in her house. Mother Mary, too, learnt through a dream about the impending birth of Christ. There are innumerable such instances of prophetic dreams.

Often, people have come up with innovative solutions in their dreams. Kekule's benzene structure, Mendelyeev's periodic table, Howe's sewing machine, Neils Bohr's model of the atom and Gandhiji's Dandi March were all ideas that had their genesis in dreams. Many scientists, inventors and technologists have literally dreamt up solutions which they could not arrive at in the waking state.

How does the mind produce such prophetic dreams? During dreaming, sensory inputs are blocked and the ego-sense 'I' is absent. This allows free reign to random thought patterns, emanating from existing memories from different parts of the brain, which produce dreams. The dreaming process therefore follows the Maxwellian distribution (the bell curve), where a majority dream about a day's events or activities. Scientists claim that the day's learning process is consolidated in our memory during sleep. This dreaming process sometimes produces disjointed dreams and at other times, nightmares. Sometimes, however, the brain synchronizes random thoughts into a powerful single thought.

Imagine hundred billion neurons of the brain synchronizing in a laser-like fashion to produce a higher dimensional thought signature. This thought connects us to a higher dimensional space-time continuum from which we get the knowledge and powers of clairvoyance. The probability of this type of synchronization is very small but it is there.

Can we deliberately produce prophetic solution dreams? Since the ever present director — the ego sense 'I' — is absent during the dreaming process, we have no control over our dreams. We can, however, control our day's events which are ultimately reflected in our dreams. Yogis claim that non-REM or dreamless sleep is possible. This is achieved through *sanyam* or contemplation and reflection and *samadhi* or focused deep meditation. Scientists, too, have discovered that REM and non-REM sleep are totally dependent on how active the brain is during daytime. The MRI brain scans of sleeping volunteers show that most of the dreaming activity takes place in the region of the brain which was most active during the daytime. Non-REM or slow-wave dreamless sleep occupies the central position in the sleep process, when information and memory consolidation process takes place. Hence REM sleep is simply a mechanism for the brain to check whether memory consolidation has taken place. Besides, it also helps us remember dreams.

So to produce happy, productive dreams, you need to be active mentally and physically — in a positive way — during waking hours.

# Ramayana's Tips for Good Governance

Pramod Pathak & Saumya Singh

he *Ramayana,* the saga of Rama's life written by Valmiki, is widely acclaimed as among the greatest of all Indian epics. The *Ramayana* can serve as a useful reference book for those willing to learn. With Rama Rajya as a model for good governance, the *Ramayana* is a must read for practitioners of statecraft.

The Ayodhya Kanda, the second chapter, contains comprehensive lessons on good governance. When Bharata, the younger brother of Rama, goes to meet the latter in the forest to request him to return to Ayodhya and rule, the two brothers enter into a long and instructive dialogue.

Rama counsels Bharata on governance. From quality of ministers and the importance of strategy sessions, to temperance in administration to justice, Rama expounds on all the subtleties of statecraft in a lucid manner. Apparently, Rama seems to be inquiring of Bharata his well-being, whether all is well at Ayodhya — in fact, however, in the process, the lessons on effective governance are offered in a powerful manner. Though the dialogue between the two brothers runs into several pages and a thorough reading is required to understand the intricacies, some important lessons are obvious, particularly the ones given on pages 441-449 of the *Valmiki Ramayana.*

A critical factor in good governance is the quality of ministers. Rama asks Bharata whether he has appointed courageous, knowledgeable, strong-willed men with a high emotional quotient as his ministers, because quality advice is the key to effective governance. The emphasis is on competence and confidentiality.

Rama's advice to Bharata is to take a decision on a complex issue neither unilaterally nor in consultation with too many people. There should be an efficient core group.

A good administrator can ensure high returns from minimum investments. Rama tells Bharata to prefer one wise man to a thousand fools as it is the wise who can ensure prosperity during an economic crisis. Even if there is one minister who is really effective, the king will gain immensely. Appointing tested men of noble lineage and integrity for strategic positions is the key to successful government. Moderate taxes should be levied on the people, lest they revolt. Rama wants Bharata to treat his soldiers well and pay their legitimate wages on time. Delays in payment of wages and other allowances can lead to dangerous consequences. Trade and agriculture are important and Rama wants Bharata to ensure good irrigation facilities rather than being overly dependent on rains. Traders need to be ensured of a fear-free environment and their grievances should be redressed promptly.

Protecting the forests and maintaining livestock have also been dealt with as important aspects of effective governance. In fact, the vision of the *Ramayana* has eternal relevance. Law and justice, finance and business, corruption framing of innocents for monetary gains, injustice to the poor are all mentioned.

Rama's words of advice to Bharata are as relevant today as they were in the Treta period, the time when Rama is believed to have lived. It is worthwhile to ponder over the thoughts and deeds of Rama rather than expend valuable time and energy fighting over his birthplace and whether a temple should be constructed there.

For the benefit of present and future generations, Rama gave valuable tips to Bharata on good governance. We should focus on this aspect rather than on outward worship.

# Take Responsibility for Your Actions

Sadhu Vishwamurtidas

ne of the most difficult and painful things to do in life is to admit one's mistakes.

When Neil Armstrong set foot on the moon the first words he meant to say and which he had practised several times were: "That's a small step for a man, but a giant leap for mankind." What he actually uttered was a contradiction: "That's a small step for man but a giant leap for mankind." But no one has acknowledged this error so far.

Most of us hesitate to confess our mistakes. We are equally reluctant to express regret, and it is a rare person who tries to make amendments or even simply render a heartfelt apology.

It is this reluctance of most people to admit that they've committed a mistake that forms the root of much human strife. An unforgiving, unrepentant nature — whether among individuals, families, communities or nations — is responsible for misunderstandings that lead to enmity and hatred.

Asked what she thought was most needed in the coming century, the celebrated historian Barbara Tuchman and Pulitzer prize winner said, "Personal responsibility... taking responsibility for your behaviour and not forever supposing that society must forgive you because it's not your fault." The mistake may not be totally one's own. But usually, in some subtle way — either through action, reaction or even inaction — we played our role poorly.

A teenager had just passed his driving test and was eager to drive his father's car. His father agreed. He asked his son to drop him at a place that was some 18 miles from home before he took the car for servicing. The father then wanted his son to pick him up at four in the afternoon so that they could go home together.

The boy dropped off his father, took the car to the garage and went to watch a film. Losing track of time, he continued to watch the film until 6pm.

Afraid his father would scold him for being late and would never give him the car again, the boy collected the car, arrived at the appointed place and said, "Dad, I'm sorry I'm late but it took the mechanic longer than usual to service the car."

"Son. I phoned the garage," his father replied. "The car was ready at 4pm." The boy looked down.

"I'm sorry, but I went to watch a film."

"Son, I'm very angry," replied the father after a moment of thought. "But not with you. I'm angry with myself. Where did I go wrong as a father? Why did you have to lie to me? Take the car home. I will introspect as I walk back."

The boy trailed behind his father, imploring him to sit inside the car. But his father continued walking silently, soul-searching all the way back home. Distraught, the son pledged to never again lie to his parents.

In the story, not only the boy, his father, too, gets transformed. We all need to examine ourselves inside — have we gone wrong somewhere? For, it is almost impossible to change others, but we can change ourselves. If we all decided to do just that, there would be no need to change anybody else anyway. The world would be transformed in a single blow.

Another thing that we need to change is our negative attitude to life. So few seem to be truly happy. Happiness is relative. It has little to do with money, fame or power. Why else do so many people who have all three end up leading miserable lives? A positive attitude will make you grow. You will be able to achieve happiness and spread it around, making the world a better place to live in.

# A Tale of Loyalty, Betrayal & Faith

### KR Narayanaswamy

here are many ways of looking at the *Ramayana*. The most instructive approach would be to focus on the epic's basic unifying theme — of loyalty and betrayal. This theme is evident in all the three categories of protagonists — the *naras*, the *vanaras* and the *rakshasas*.

Prominent among the *nara* loyalists are Lakshmana and Bharata. Lakshmana's loyalty to Rama is total and unconditional, but highly personalized. But he doesn't share Rama's passion for *dharma*. He even suspects collusion between his father and stepmother, and even Bharata of hostile designs. And he is willing to take on Dasaratha, Kaikeyi, Bharata, the whole of Ayodhya to secure for his brother what is rightfully his — his kingdom.

Bharata is just as loyal to Rama as his younger brother but his loyalty is firmly grounded in *dharma*. Unlike Lakshmana, Bharata has a mind of his own and speaks out fearlessly, no matter who is at the receiving end — his mother, his preceptor Vashista or Rama himself. Shaken to the core by what his mother has done, he goes to where his brother is to bring him back. When he fails in his mission, he returns to the outskirts of Ayodhya, enthrones Rama's sandals, and rules for the next 14 years as Rama's representative. He also follows an austere lifestyle to match that of his exiled brother. Bharata's self-denial is legendary — many Vaishnava devotees from the south regard him as the real hero of the *Ramayana*.

Among the *rakshasa* loyalists are Vibhishana and Kumbhakarna. Vibhishana is devoted to *dharma* and so to Rama, the embodiment of *dharma*.

However, his kind of loyalty is not universally appreciated. Some consider him a traitor who betrayed his brother and crossed over to join the enemy camp, an opportunist who espouses the winning cause. He was so unlike his brother Kumbhakarna, who chooses to fight on Ravana's side knowing fully well that he and his brother both are fated to die. He refuses to desert his blood brother even

128

though he knows Ravana is in the wrong. Confucius would have approved.

On being told of a son who bore witness against a guilty father, the Chinese sage is said to have remarked, "In our part of the country the son would shield his guilty father." Hanuman is foremost among the *vanara* loyalists. He lives and breathes only to serve Rama. He is prepared to face any danger or adverse situation, fight against enemies and do anything, all in the service of Rama. A redoubtable warrior and a consummate diplomat among other things, Hanuman is presented convincingly by Valmiki.

Sugreeva, the monkey king, begins as a trusted ally of Rama but soon becomes his 'dasa'. However, his role vis-a-vis his brother Vali is ambivalent, somewhat like Vibhishana's vis-a-vis Ravana.

On what ground does he conclude that the blood that he sees gushing out of the cave-mouth is Vali's and not the demon Mayavi's as the two slug it out inside the cave? The poet doesn't tell us.

What makes Sugreeva seal the entrance to the cave with a huge rock before returning to Kishkinda with the tale of Vali's death?

Is he driven by desire to usurp the throne of Vali? Stricken by the sight of a brother bleeding to death and caught in an orgiastic bout of remorse and self-accusation, Sugreeva himself says so, while Vali for his part is inclined to take more of the blame on himself. The poet, it would seem, blames both the brothers, one for yielding to *kama*, the other to *krodha*.

# Krishna & Kaliya: Good Fights Evil

Amishi Dhanuka

t is a universal law: If we have ego, we will suffer. If we are arrogant, again, we will suffer till we are forced to surrender. The subduing of Kaliya the serpent by Krishna illustrates this.

The tenth canto of the Srimad Bhagvatam recounts the Kaliya *daman lila* performed by Krishna. Kaliya was a venomous serpent that lived in the Yamuna river. One summer Krishna's cowherd friends fainted and died when they drank water from the Yamuna. Kaliya had contaminated the river so much that vapour from the river was lethal enough to kill birds flying across.

When Krishna saw his transcendental companions die, he jumped into the river and agitated the water like a large thunderous elephant. Kaliya was filled with *amrsyama-nah* (intolerance and rage) at the presence of the trespasser. He took Krishna captive in his coils and raised his 101 heads. Krishna allowed him to do so for a while as he stayed still. Everyone standing on the banks of the river was very afraid and anxious except Balaram who was quietly smiling in full knowledge of Krishna's potential.

As Krishna observed his mother Yashoda faint on the banks, he quickly began to expand his form to proportions beyond Kaliya's control. Kaliya lost his grip on Krishna and the Lord, standing on Kaliya's head, began to dance. With every rise and fall of his rhythmic steps, the serpent became more and more bewildered and overpowered. Weakened and powerless, Kaliya was now at Krishna's mercy. It was the prayer of Kaliya's pious wives, the *nagapatnis*, that saved him from annihilation. As a helpless and battered Kaliya began to chant prayers to Krishna, he promised to surrender at the Lord's feet. Krishna granted the transformed Kaliya forgiveness.

Kaliya symbolizes many aspects of Kaliyug. Kaliya is black, the colour symbolizing demoniac characteristics very similar to the inherent nature of contemporary man who is devious, proud, arrogant and envious. Kaliya imagines himself to be invincible, like many of us do today as we glow in the deceptive light of our false ego. Kaliya is also materially attached. He thinks he is the king of the Yamuna river. We think we are masters of the universe.

Kaliya's body is slimy and slippery, very like his personality. An opportunist, he tries every trick to bite Krishna. Kaliya is a control freak. He is ignorant and *tamasic* to the core. He has a terrible temper and spews venom incessantly. Kaliya had so many heads that it is impossible for him to have any clarity of thought — they are symbols of confusion.

If the above characteristics sound too far-fetched to be a part of our ethos, think again. Each one of us has these negativities whether we accept them or not. To rise above them, to become pure, you need to surrender unto the creator like Kaliya did. Because real peace and happiness can be experienced only when one is pure, not when one is contaminated. And we have contaminated our existence by constantly drinking the poison of materialistic existence. And that poison kills our propensity to be happy.

Every time we speak an unnecessary word, or do something to take us towards more materialism, we are actually behaving like a serpent spewing venom. Our ego and pride are stumbling blocks on our path to spiritual progress. Subduing our innate sense of arrogance by unconditionally surrendering to the creator is the only way to experience bliss. The story of Krishna and Kaliya the snake is the story of how, ultimately, good triumphs over evil.

# Good Thoughts, Words, Deeds & More

Ervad Marzban Hathiram

ach and every creation of the supreme Lord Ahura Mazda has been given a specific divine task, to be performed at various stages of existence. Yet caught in the whirlwind of daily life, we tend to forget our responsibilities, distracted by worldly pursuits.

Our actions spurred by our weaknesses take us even further away from God, deadening the mind to our ultimate goal, salvation.

How should we concentrate on our spiritual responsibilities without losing track of our secular liabilities? The Zoroastrian scriptures offer the solution in following the practice of Meher-Patet. Meher signifies absolute truth, and Patet, the practice of immediate and public acceptance of a wrongdoing. How does this help?

Meher is also the Yazata or divine entity connected with the sun's rays. The rays of the sun engulf the entire earth and every atom of our body craves for the life-giving properties of the sun. When we follow the practice of Meher-Patet, the life force of Meher present in the sun's rays is infused into our body and alerts our consciousness towards spiritual responsibilities. Thus roused, we become open to Meher Yazata.

Meher Yazata sows the seeds of goodness in us, enriching our soul with physical, mental and spiritual wellness, enabling us to reap the fruits of our hard work. We become aware that our deeds must not be just those driven by our personal needs, but should rise to the level of Hvarshta or good deeds which fulfil the divine task entrusted to him by his maker.

Once we convert our deeds to Hvarshta, we become associates of nature, attempting to help other entities in their divine tasks. As we understand more and more of the mysterious working of nature we realize the magnitude of the task entrusted to us. We observe the

132

working of the Celestial Ones and decide to sing their praise. We get more conscious of what and how we speak, ultimately speaking less and praising the work of the divine ones through the Mantras more.

By controlling our tongue, we are able to advance to the level of Hukhta or good words — that is, words which when spoken have the effect of immediately delivering what they promise. As we attain the stage of Hukhta, we come into direct contact with the Divine. We realize that all of creation works according to the Ahuna Vairya: The Divine Thought and Will of Ahura Mazda.

Our entire mind becomes focused on how to further the Will of the Creator. We realize the futility of harbouring other thoughts, and hence begins the process of cleansing our mind and thought process.

After long practice and divine help, we gain control of the mind, removing all extraneous thoughts from it, replacing them with just one central and over-arching thought: 'How shall I further the Will of Ahura Mazda?'

As our mind gets cleansed, it becomes the abode of Vohu Mana: the 'good enlightened mind', and our thoughts transcend the temporal and attain the state of Humata or 'good thoughts'.

This is the real meaning of the oft-quoted phrase Humata, Hukhta and Hvarshta, wrongly used to describe the so-called adage of the Zoroastrian religion: good thoughts, good words and good deeds.

Since our current thoughts, words and deeds are far from reaching that state of perfection, we need to adopt the path shown by Prophet Zarathushtra: cultivating the habit of truthfulness at all times, and deve-loping the moral courage to publicly accept our failure when we get diverted from this difficult practice.

# Celebrate Life with Sankalpa Yoga

## Mahayogi Pilot Baba

ankalpa Yoga is 'reso-will', the power that is born of resolve, will and determination. This esoteric yogic science was widely practised 5,000 years ago. But the misuse of the power of Sankalpa Yoga led to a great deal of destruction. Over time, this form of yoga slipped into oblivion, but it was preserved and guarded by Himalayan masters. Now there is renewed interest in the subject, and it is believed that its revival will empower mankind to achieve peace and goodwill.

Sankalpa Yoga is a sacred science of the Himalayas, practised from time immemorial by enlightened people like Kashyapa, Atri, Vyasa, Dattatreya, Rama, Krishna and others. By leading the practitioner towards liberation, this form of yoga allows him to return to that state of consciousness that comes through *samadhi*, and brings with it the power and determination to change our thought vibrations.

The Himalayan masters have recognized that man has lost the way to himself, and has lost the key to harmony and balance. The world is threatened by negative energies that have been cultivated in an insatiable greed for power. Religion is no longer a unifying force; it is now being used as a means to manipulate people. Power and control are the operative principles of today's ethos. The traditions of the past have been thrown away, and we have no universal values to replace them.

We are afraid — the web of *karmas* we have got entangled in have instilled these fears in us. We are afraid of war, disease, society, of each other and ourselves; we're afraid of living as well as of dying. We have gone too far away from ourselves to remember who we are, to remember that we came in joy, to live in joy, to serve a higher purpose — to manifest the pure light of consciousness.

The Himalayan masters are willing to share the secrets by which the world can be changed and positive energy can be transmitted to liberate humanity from forces of destruction. They want to share with you the power of transformation — to rediscover your spirituality which will lead you to awareness and joy.

The key to the secrets of the universe is available through *samadhi* which leads you to yourself. *Samadhi* undertaken with *sankalpa* has the power to create universal consciousness. The Mahabharata war was once fought and won with the help of *sankalpa shakti*.

To experience liberation, you have to be free from bondage, which is nothing but an outcome of your thoughts. Sankalpa Yoga leads to realization, which brings liberation — freedom from all bondage. Life is to enjoy and to celebrate. This enjoyment and celebration is possible through the practice of Sankalpa Yoga, which can take you to living beyond consciousness. It allows you to live in this world with knowledge of the world and knowledge born of wisdom.

Sankalpa Yoga is the science of creation. Like everything in nature, *gyana* (knowledge) comes through *sankalpa*. Sankalpa Yoga does not belong to anyone in particular, nor is it registered by any organization. It belongs to all those who want to practise it. There is no one to command you, no bondage, no milestones. You have to find a new path. You are not part of history; you are part of the present.

You can empower yourself with knowledge through the ancient and sacred art of Sankalpa Yoga, by learning the techniques that enable meditation. One has to practice with determination, tirelessly. Open your heart so that you may receive. Prepare yourself for Divine grace. Dive deep within yourself and you will recognize yourself — you will be free.

# Elephant & the Monk:
# Story of Compassion

Sudhamahi Regunathan

nce there lived a strong, young elephant named Meruprabh. One day a part of a huge forest caught fire and the fire spread rapidly, fanned by strong winds. The animals were scared. When would the fire stop? Meruprabh along with 700 other elephants cleared one part of the forest of vegetation to prevent the fire from spreading. This clearing became a haven for animals seeking shelter from the fire and they huddled there till the fire went out. Animals who normally hunted each other now sat or stood close in amity. Fear was palpable.

Soon this clearing was so full that there was no space for even a grain of sesame. Packed it was, in both space and tension. At that time as Meruprabh also stood, he felt his knee itch. He had to scratch himself. He lifted the other leg and scratched himself. What a relief it was! Scratching, he reflected, was one of the pleasures of life.

But no sooner had he afforded himself a little pleasure he looked down to find a little rabbit scurrying into the space that had been cleared when he lifted his leg. Breathing heavily the rabbit snuggled into the space. What happens to Meruprabh's leg? As he held it above the ground, he realized that if he put it down, he would crush the rabbit. Could he nudge the rabbit to a side? Oh no, there was simply no space. Meruprabh folded his leg and decided to hold it there rather than hurt the hapless frightened creature.

One day and night passed. The forest fire was still raging. The animals did not move. Not even Meruprabh. He kept standing with one leg folded.

The second and third day too passed. Finally the flames subsided and the animals venturing out cautiously in the beginning ran out to see if it were safe to return to their homes. Only Meruprabh continued to stand. His leg had become stiff and he could not put it down now. When he tried to straighten it, he felt a shooting pain and losing his balance, he tumbled over. He lay there like that for a long time till he quietly succumbed to it.

"No being is to be harmed for all beings desire to live and no one wishes to die," Mahavira taught his followers. For his exemplary act of compassion Meruprabh earned the privilege of being born a king in his next birth and in that very same birth, he eventually became a monk. This story is related when prince Megha, ordained as a monk with permission from his parents, enters the *ashram*. He spends a very uncomfortable night. The floor is hard for the prince who was accustomed to velvet beds. It is cold too. Moreover, all the senior monks are up and about even in the late hours of the night. They give him room in a corridor and so he gets disturbed when each of them passes by. Night seemed endless and finally at daybreak the newly initiated monk went to his teacher. He stood there, speechless. He wanted to leave. He wanted to go home.

The minutes ticked by. The teacher, watching his discomfort, said, "Go child and get back to work. Do not give up so easily. This discomfort is nothing as compared to what you faced in your last birth when you were not even a human being. You gave up your life in compassion, today you fret about a small pain? Because you exhibited such extraordinary compassion you were able to be born as a prince and even attained monkhood. Now enjoy the fruits of your good deeds." The monk, gaining new insight and realizing the gift of his birth, became one of the most sincere disciples of the *sangha*.

# Drawing Inspiration from Playing Fields

## Kiran Bedi

nnual sports functions are quite similar in the choice of events and the manner in which they are conducted. But the one I attended recently was different, for purely personal reasons.

While viewing the events, my mind began exploring and searching for hidden messages behind each performance. I wondered whether the children and their parents, for whom all this was being enacted, were aware of the spirit behind the sporting events. Could it be that the teachers, who conceptualized and organized the events, deliberately structured them in such a way as to make the participants more aware persons?

I had no prepared speech; so I decided to take the children on an internal journey. After I thanked the school authorities for inviting me, I asked the students, did they really want to hear a speech?

"Yes," they chorused.

I said, "In that case, you will need to come close to me to be in eye contact." This meant children who were spread out in the field would need to move closer. And they did. The students and I were now in eye contact. I was standing on a platform which was four feet high. To begin with, I made them all sit up and asked them to say "Jai Hind." I then asked them if they would like to take home a treasure. At first, they responded in a cautious manner as they did not know what I meant. I asked them again if I could offer them a treasure to take home and keep forever. They said, "Yes." "Then listen to me carefully and look at me," I said. I asked them if they knew there was a hidden treasure in all the events which they had performed that morning. I said, "You began with a display of karate. Do you know what it means?"

They all replied, "Self-defence!"

"Of course, but what more?" I asked.

They looked at me, puzzled. I explained to them that karate gave them courage, fitness, self-sufficiency and self-dependence, all of which is crucial for self-defence. "You do not practise karate only for self-defence — in the process, you learn courage, physical fitness, confidence and self-sufficiency which then enable you to defend yourself ably. Self-defence is not just a physical act, it is your whole self — your mind, your body and your spirit," I said to them.

Did they understand what I was trying to say? Some, apparently, did understand the larger dimensions of learning. I then moved on to the next treasure I thought they could carry home. I referred to the march past and asked them if they knew why was it so good. I told them what I thought. It was because they had all rehearsed together for many days as a team with a leader who was the best amongst them. They obeyed the right commands with trust and respect. They were focused. They were not absent-minded. So what is the treasure, I asked them. The children came up with various answers: Practice, teamwork, leadership, concentration, hard work.

On a lighter note, I asked them if they knew why their parents had lost the tug-of-war game to the teachers. "Is it because you all rooted for them or was it because teachers were united and cohesive?" I asked.

"Unity," they chorused.

I went on to tell them that when we all work together with a plan, we prepare, rehearse and are focused, so we can succeed.

School sporting events are, in fact, symbolic of the values we need to follow in our lives. These are not rituals; they are demonstrations that inculcate right values in us from childhood, to be nurtured and integrated.

And it is this aspect which children need to be told about. This could be an interesting and inspiring resolve with which to begin the new year — to look beyond events and happenings to understand the real meaning of life, and so add value to our lives.

# The Fine Art of Wise Parenting

Swami Sukhabodhananda

hildren are very creative. However, when faced with failure, they might become dispirited. Good parenting can enable children to accept facts of life and persuade them to proceed proactively in a creative mode. The challenge of life is in accepting the fact that 'life is not fair'. Once you accept this fact, a certain understanding is generated. This will enable you to accept whatever life gives you.

Life is unfair. One child is born physically challenged while another is born healthy. Only when we begin to accept life can we understand it. You are born in a poor family. Accept it. Use whatever life gives you. You will find that acceptance leads to creativity. Teach the child to use whatever life has given. Give examples of creative people who have faced challenges. Helen Keller was left sightless and with impaired hearing after an illness when she was barely six years old. Yet, she gained fame as a great social worker. Poet John Milton had lost his eye-sight before he wrote his masterpiece, *Paradise Lost*.

Every moment is the best; live life with this attitude. Be in the present where there is a hidden message, a mystery, and a possibility. Accept them and allow the magic to flow. Acceptance is not resigning to what is, but allowing what is, so as to gain empowerment and guidance. But simply accepting without creativity is resignation. Life should be a balance between creativity and acceptance. Every parent should see whether the child's balance of Shiva and Shakti, or male and female energy — creativity and acceptance — is there. Once there is balance, the energy field helps the child live wisely. He will use whatever life gives him rather than being used by life. This is the insight every parent should gift to his or her children.

Parents should motivate children to identify a powerful goal; to learn to be a winner both in the inner and outer sphere. The outer winner achieves success. The inner winner gains satisfaction. A child should learn to be successful; he also has to learn to be satisfied. Striking a balance between success and satisfaction is important.

"Success is getting what I like; satisfaction is liking what I get."
Success does not equal satisfaction. Our desires should be sacred,
not sensuous. Our desires should be twofold: one pointing outward
and the other, pointing inward. The outward desire should be to
contribute to the world. The inward desire should be to learn from
any given situation and grow. But desire has no end. You may be
successful, but if your mind is filled with desire, you can never be
happy. Children, teenagers, even parents, make the mistake of
thinking: "Success is the only vision in life." Good parenting should
involve guiding the child to not just learn to get what he likes but
also learn to like what he gets.

Our scriptures talk about pleasure and pain. *Sukha prapti* is
acquisition of happiness and *dukha nivritti* is putting an end to
unhappiness. If *sukha* (pleasure) and *dukha* (pain) are perceived
wisely, temptations to smoke and drink, for instance, will be treated
as pain. But, the mind treats it as pleasure — hence you indulge
yourself.

You can train your mind and say it is pain. 'Not smoking' is
pleasure. 'Why?' 'By not smoking' you will be healthy; you can live
better and longer. The moment you represent it as *prati paksha
bhavana*, you are reversing the whole thing, and then you will find
that you have the skill to handle any temptation in life. Therefore,
parents should teach children to use the techniques of pleasure and
pain in an intelligent way.

# Don't go to Seed, be a Karmayogi

## BR Sood

ndian philosophical tradition presents various ways and means of orchestrating the thought process to quieten down the mind. These methods do yield positive results to those who adopt, practice and follow these tenets. However, there is a misconception that a person who puts in efforts to still the mind with the help of tips given by sacred texts eventually ends up as an ascetic. This is the basis of arguments against religious practices — that in a world full of ascetics, no activity, be it agriculture, industry or governance, could ever function at its best.

These arguments go a step further to suggest that new ideas and ideal solutions to complicated problems emanate from restless minds. Nevertheless the best counter to such erroneous arguments is contained in the *Bhagavad Gita* where the Lord advises Arjuna to be a *karmayogi*; a person who performs all the duties to his or her maximum potential and capability without any attachment and without expecting rewards. Being dispassionate while performing one's duty helps one to maintain mental balance while being engrossed completely in one's profession.

Modern day professionalism is nothing but *karma yoga* at its best. True professionals obtain the best possible training necessary for the job to be executed with precision and perfection, and in an efficient manner. Once the objectives of the job to be performed have been understood clearly and matched with the person's capability, capacity to work and training and there is willingness to put in all that there is into performing the job, the satisfaction and calmness one obtains more than compensates for the energy expended in doing the job. A job well done without hassles is a reward in itself.

However, those who view their job as a drudgery often end up making a complete mess of the assigned job, which leads to mental disturbance. The old adage 'A bad workman finds fault with his tools' comes true for such persons who keep on finding excuses and blaming others for their own lack of efficiency and will power.

A parable that brings out clearly the role of performing the assigned job with full concentration in quietening the mind goes like this: In the *ashram* of an enlightened sage a number of disciples were undergoing training. One disciple, in whom the sage saw the potential of the makings of a great man, was assigned the boring and routine duty of grinding sesame seeds in the kitchen. Since sesame seeds formed a part of everyone's diet in the *ashram*, this disciple had to spend whole of his time grinding the seeds. He accepted the assigned duty with pleasure and put in all efforts to grind the necessary quantity of seeds daily as best as he could without any thought about the task being a very routine one. Years went by and the sage let this disciple do the grinding undisturbed while other students were taught various subjects.

Finally the sage decided to appoint one of the disciples to take his place and look after the activities of the *ashram* so that he himself could now retire. All the disciples were asked to come up with a great philosophical thought and pen it down. The one who came up with the best thought would take over the reins of the *ashram*. Only the best amongst the lot — except the grinder — dared to write such a thought. "The mind is like a mirror and thoughts act like dust on the mirror. Occasionally it is necessary to remove dust from the mirror" wrote the student. The idea sounded good and everybody was convinced that the author of this novel idea would be choice of the sage.

Disciples engaged in discussing the idea went to the kitchen and the disciple who had been grinding the seeds in the kitchen for years together started laughing uncontrollably at the great philosophical thought enunciated by the 'best' of the lot. When asked why he was laughing, his simple reply was "What mirror and what dust?" He had been so engrossed in executing the duty assigned to him that no thought other than the thought of doing his duty well ever entered his mind. And that gave him the power to keep his mind quiet. He was chosen to succeed the sage.

Doing one's job skilfully, efficiently and with full concentration is yoga. This point made in ancient Indian philosophical thought is the guiding philosophy and driving force behind today's professionalism. Those who devote themselves completely to their duty would not have the time to ponder over irrelevant thoughts that keep the mind agitated. This is the essence of *karma yoga*.

# Change Your Life with Zero Draft

Susrut Ray

ears ago George K taught me the zero draft technique. I was what they call a 'first time manager' — a techie who has served his time in the labs and who is taking his first plunge into the real and complex world of people, money and markets. I was to make a plan — a 'pilot production plan' for a new product. Like any typical ex-techie I was lost. How does one go about making a plan? What is a plan anyway? Outwardly I was scornful of the whole idea.

I still remember the neat little lecture that George K delivered: "What is a plan, why one needs to have one, how one goes about making a plan. He whipped out a fresh sheet of paper, wrote on top of it in block letters 'Plan for the production of model X'."

He neatly folded it and gave it to me. "That's how you get started. That's your zero draft. Now get cracking." For the next 48 hours I kept jotting down whatever came to my mind about the production. On the third day I put a structure to my jottings. I had made my first formal plan.

I have used the Zero Draft Technique (ZDT) for a quarter of a century. Whenever I was in a fuzzy situation the ZDT came in handy. I silently thanked George and wondered how a plain sheet could make all the difference. Reflecting on this, I concluded that when you want to do something, you always start from zero point.

In the beginning is an intention. You can't touch or physically hold an intention, so in a sense it is hardly real. You have now to realize your intention. How? You have to make a plan. How do you begin? Logicians call problems associated with 'getting started' as problems that sprout from 'infinite regress'. It is one of the two big monsters logicians have learned to steer clear of — the other is that monster of self-contradiction. You have to cut out of the regress at the very beginning. When you write down your 'intention' on a piece of paper, you have the beginnings of your plan, your zero draft. Only the details need to be filled in.

You have reserved a space, the blank sheet you may call the form.

144

You have put in a little content, too. The nearest natural phenomenon I can use as a metaphor to explain the effect is the growth of a crystal. You need to insert one little crystal into a solution of sugar to make a candy. It is the same with thoughts.

A plan is a conglomeration of large numbers of little thoughts which float around in the mind space. Give them a little platform to land on. It is then simpler to organize them. How do you proceed beyond the blank sheet? Typically one would start by filling it in with items like 'production start date', 'target date of completion' and so on. Each in itself is quite meaningless. Each has to have a value or a content. Form and content together make up the plan.

The zero draft represents to me a truth which goes far beyond mere planning or execution. It represents a basic format for understanding life itself. Life and its products have to be seen as the union of two parts: little things and their organization.

Bricks are not houses, nor are wooden boards chairs. Plan and execution, thought and action, form and content in eternal braids are the threads that life is made of. Most importantly, there has to be the beginnings of a braiding process somewhere — there has to be a zero draft.

The grandest example of the braiding process is, of course, the beginnings of life itself. Matter and purpose in eternal collaboration created life. In the beginning there was just matter with no purpose. Then the deoxyribonucleic acid molecule, the celebrated DNA, appeared. It was a molecule with a purpose; an interest in self-replication. That was the beginning, the zero draft. In our current understanding of human knowledge yet again I hear echoes of the braiding process. The two parts of knowledge are sense data and the categories or pigeon holes to put the sense data into.

Great as he was as a mentor, George K knew none of this. I often wonder how much more effective he would have been if he did. But logicians and philosophers, barring a few exceptions, seldom pay much attention to application of their theories. They are more concerned with depth and correctness. As a result, their language gets stilted far beyond the reach of the average production manager. That is a pity, for theory and practice ought to work together intertwined like the rest of them. That alone can make a meaningful whole.

# Inspiring Tales of True Conversion

## Seema Burman

ugustine was a renowned intellectual of the fourth century. But he had his vices; and was particularly fond of drinking alcohol. He tried hard to overcome his bad habits. He constantly prayed to the Lord, but in vain. His mother Monica too prayed to Jesus to help him. In *Confessions*, St Augustine describes how he would plead to God: 'O Lord! How long am I to wait for this change? How long? How long? Tomorrow, tomorrow; why not today? Why not now? Why not this very hour see the end of my wretchedness?' It was a prayer from the heart and miraculously, Augustine was converted from a life of vices to a life of moderation and spirituality.

Swami Ranganathananda of the Ramakrishna Mission says that when a soul is uplifted, a worthwhile conversion takes place that takes the soul vertically upward — from bad to good. This conversion benefits both the individual and society. Organized religion has two sides to it: One is dogmatic, narrow, given to fanaticism, that insists on rituals, rules, regulations, disciplines. The other side, the spiritual, elevates and feeds the soul and accepts goodness in all religions. Rituals and prayers are merely means to rein in our senses to bring out our *sattvic gunas*.

Those who are obsessed with only dogma throughout their lives find that they are not respected; moreover, no change for the better is perceived in them. Hindu tradition respects those who experience the infinite Existence-Knowledge-Absolute Bliss or *Satchidananda* irrespective of their religion, caste or creed.

When spirituality is discernible no further questions are asked. Spirituality cannot be labelled as belonging to a particular religion, sect or cult. A 'religious' person sports outward symbols like holy marks on forehead, dress and religious symbols. A spiritual person might not follow any of these; he might not even be articulate, but is constantly under the spell of divine bliss, he loves entire humankind, accepts all and respects every religion. Sanatana

Dharma calls such a one as an avatar.

Valmiki was a dacoit. Yet, he rose to the divine stage of *Satchidananda*. Sita took shelter in his cottage and her twin sons, Luv and Kush, were brought up by this dacoit-turned-saint. His creation, the *Ramayana* in Sanskrit, was the first-ever narration of Rama's life. Rama himself was the first listener, and Luv-Kush were the first narrators. Valmiki's conversion from dacoit to peace-loving sage was accepted by other sages without prejudice.

Tulsidas is another example of the miracle of conversion. He was ridiculed and rebuked by his wife. Fed up, she advised him to develop such intense devotion towards God which could lead him ultimately to realization of God. Overnight, Tulsidas turned all his energies towards Rama. His devotion led to his writing the *Ramcharitmanas* and he was blessed none other than Rama and Lakshmana at Chitrakoot.

Emperor Ashoka, the fearsome warrior, one day dropped his weapons and adopted *ahimsa* or non-violence as his mantra, after witnessing the bloodshed and death at Kalinga.

So the mind has tremendous potential. Anyone can turn the mind's direction from one extreme to another. So conversion is something that's private — it happens inside the person undergoing an intense inner transformation. Conversion is meaningful only when a person becomes spiritually evolved. That is a great achievement.

In all traditions, there exist opportunities for one to become a better person, of changing one's outlook. Every religion has produced great saints and sages and what we need today are not caste fights but a collaboration at the spiritual level. What we need is a pooling of spiritual resources to bring about universal harmony.

# Selfless Labour is Karma Yoga

### Parmarthi Raina

hy do we work? We work for our livelihood, to provide for our family and contribute to society. Often, we wonder what the real purpose of human life is. Vedic scriptures tell us that it is *moksha*, or liberation from the cycle of birth and death.The *Bhagavad Gita* recommends four yogas — *karma* (action or work), *raja* (meditation), *jnana* (knowledge) and *bhakti* (devotion) — as paths to achieve this goal. Of these, *karma yoga* is the most practical.

The *Gita* says that if we do our *svadharma*, duty, correctly and as per the four *varnas*, which are *brahmana, kshatriya, vaishya* and *shudra*, we can attain perfection. The classification of the *varnas*, applicable to all mankind, is based on an individual's nature and character, which in turn is believed to be formed by the three *gunas* of *prakriti* or modes of material nature. However, with the passage of time, the *varnashrama* system was perverted and duties came to be assigned according to *varnas* sub-divided into castes on a hereditary basis.

In today's competitive world, finding a profession based on one's *svadharma* is not the norm. The tendency is to work for the highest remuneration, or to do whatever work one gets in this era of growing unemployment, even if it is incompatible with one's nature and disposition. So whatever work one is doing can be accepted as *svadharma*. The *Gita* says that all occupations are equally good, be they of a *sanyasi* or householder, of a judge or sweeper, and when performed to the best of one's ability and without attachment, help in advancing on the spiritual path.

Generally, we work for personal gain or satisfaction, which is a selfish motive. Selfish actions dissipate moral energy and do not promote spiritual development. *Karma yoga* is a system of ethics focused on unselfish action. According to Swami Vivekananda, that activity which is selfish is immoral, and that which is unselfish is moral. Work is never the cause of misery, selfishness is.

Vedic scriptures affirm that selfishness comes from attachment — with people, things, and to the results of one's work. It arises from a sense of possession that in turn comes from an identification with things as 'mine'. This sense of 'mine' comes from identification with one's bodily identity, wherein one thinks in terms of 'my body', 'my intelligence', 'my property', and 'my children'. In reality, none of these are ours because everything belongs to God. Non-attachment, *vairagya*, is a state of mind, rather than an external condition. A king may live in non-attachment, and a beggar in rags may be very attached to his meagre possessions.

One must strive to attain a state of detachment where one seeks nothing, not even reward or praise, for any of one's actions and remains unaffected equally by the good and the bad. We are not, and cannot be, the architects of the fruits of our labour.

Krishna tells Arjuna (*Gita* 2.47-50), "You have the right to perform your prescribed duty, but you are not entitled to the fruits of your actions. Never consider yourself the cause of the results of your activities, and never be attached to not doing your duty. Perform your duty with equipoise, O Arjuna, abandoning all attachments to success and failure and be equanimous in all conditions."

Selflessness in action does not come easy. One way to cultivate it is to surrender one's work unto the Lord. Krishna tells Arjuna (*Gita* 3.9), "Work has to be done as a sacrifice to God otherwise it causes bondage with this material world. Perform your prescribed duties for His satisfaction and without personal attachment." Again, in the *Gita* (9.27) he says, "Whatever you do, whatever you offer or give in charity, do it as an offering to Me."

Before Lord Krishna instructed him through the *Gita* to go ahead and perform his *svadharma*, Arjuna was attempting to escape from the situation under the pretence of becoming a renunciate.

Krishna explained to him that to abjure activity and practise workless asceticism is sheer idleness and hypocrisy. Gauging Arjuna's state of mind that made it impossible for him to do his duty, Krishna commanded him (*Gita* 3.30), "Therefore, O Arjuna, surrendering all your actions unto Me, with full knowledge of Me, without desire for profit, with no claims to proprietorship and free from lethargy, fight (do your duty)." Indeed, this is Krishna's advice to all of us, too.

# Scholar, Soldier, Saint & Poet

### Pranav Khullar

aint, scholar, soldier all rolled into one, Guru Gobind Singh was responsible for the evolution of the Khalsa Panth. He was nine years old when the dismembered head of his father Guru Teg Bahadur was brought to him at Anandpur Saheb. This became the turning point in Gobind Rai's life and paved the way for the concretization of the Sikh tradition. The child held back his tears, embraced the faithful Jaita who had risked his life to bring the sacred trust in tact, and declared that henceforth all untouchables would be the Guru's own children. Thus began the *dharam yudh* Guru Gobind Singh launched against tyranny and injustice.

Swami Vivekananda said, "The Guru lived and died for *dharma* to preserve the values of his motherland and protect the honour of his countrymen." It is said that when Swamiji narrated the tales of valour and nobility of Guru Gobind Singh to his disciples tears would well up in his eyes while the listeners were fired by the Guru's heroic deeds. In the *Zafarnama* the Guru addressed Aurangzeb thus: "A religious man never breaks his promise. You are faithless and unreligious. You know neither God nor Prophet Mohammad. What if my four sons have been killed? It is no heroism to extinguish a few sparks."

Rabindranath Tagore called Guru Gobind Singh a 'great harbinger of change' — his greatest achievement being the creation of the Khalsa, a new social order where every one is equal. This new order played the role of defending the nation, members fought like lions in war and acted as model citizens in peace. Historian Dr HR Gupta captures the etymological and philosophical/spiritual significance of each of the five letters of the Persian word, *Khalsa* — 'Kh' and 'a', stand, respectively for *Khud* or oneself and the *Akal Purkh* (God). The third letter 'l', signifies *Labbaik*, meaning the following question of God: "What do you want with me? Here I am. What would you have?" and the reply of the Singh (devotee) — "Lord give us liberty and sovereignty." The fourth letter 's' signifies *Saheb* (Lord). The last letter is written either as 'a' or, more usually, 'h'. The former signifies *azadi* or freedom and the latter refers to *Huma*, the legendary bird."

The philosophy of the Khalsa falls in line with Indian spiritual tradition which goes beyond toleration. "The Sikh Gurus who compiled the Adi Granth," says Dr Radhakrishnan, "had this noble quality of appreciation of whatever was valuable in other religious traditions." The *Guru Granth Saheb* itself is replete with verses and hymns from the Sufi traditions of Baba Farid as well as the *bhakti* tradition of Namdev and the Maharashtrian saints besides Kabir and Dhanna. Guru Gobind Singh symbolized the spiritual-moral upsurge of his times.

According to Macauliff in his *Sikh Religion, Its Guru, Sacred Writings and Authors*, Guru Gobind Singh's first sermon to his disciples is significant and clarifies all doubts about the Guru's concept of the Khalsa — "Let all embrace one creed and obliterate difference of religion. Let the four castes which have different rules for their guidance abandon them all, adopt one from the adoration and become brothers. Let no one deem himself superior to another." According to Arnold Toynbee, Guru Gobind Singh anticipated Lenin by two hundred years.

Guru Gobind Singh wrote in Punjabi, Hindi and Persian. He wrote *Dasam Granth* in Punjabi, *Hikayats* and *Zafarnama* in Persian and *Ram Avtar, Krishan Avtar* and *Bachitra Natak* in Brajbhasha. All these works are marked by a high degree of excellence and sensibility. Giani Gian Singh, author of *Tawarik-e-Guru-Khalsa* captures the spirit of the Guru when he writes "Guru Gobind Singh could snatch valuable hours from his martial activities for writing historical literature during his stay at Poanta Saheb. Tradition holds that the torrents of the river Yamuna adopted pin-drop silence when the Guru indulged in literary pursuits."

The Guru fought his *dharam yudh* in the great epical tradition of righteousness to restore the moral balance of the age: "When all other means fail, it is lawful to draw the sword," he declared. The great *karmayogi* that he was, his life and character are summed up beautifully in his own oft-quoted verse from his Chandi Charitra:

"Grant me, My Lord, the Boon
Never to falter in doing a noble deed."

# Silence of Words Inspired Osho

### Swami Chaitanya Keerti

ew books are being published every day, and millions of books are available worldwide. Still, many old books continue to remain popular because people just love reading them. The thirst for knowledge and wisdom, fiction and fun is insatiable. Once in a while we come across a book that transforms us and changes the course of our life.

Osho loved reading books and he did read more than 100,000 books, which are now part of his personal library. Osho makes a special mention of one unique book which not many people know of. He says, "There are millions of books in the world, but *The Book of Mirdad* stands out far above any other book in existence. It is unfortunate that very few people are acquainted with this book because it is not a religious scripture. It is a parable, a fiction, but containing oceanic truth. It is a small book, but the man who gave birth to this book — and mind my words, I am not saying 'the man who wrote this book', nobody wrote this book — was an unknown, a nobody. And because he was not a novelist, he never wrote again; just that single book contains his whole experience. The name of the man was Mikhail Naimy.

"It is an extraordinary book in the sense that you can read it and miss it completely, because the meaning of the book is not in the words of the book. The meaning of the book is running side by side in silence between the words, between the lines, in the gaps. If you are in a state of meditativeness — if you are not only reading a fiction but you are encountering the whole religious experience of a great human being, absorbing it; not intellectually understanding but existentially drinking it — the words are there but they become secondary. Something else becomes primary: the silence that those words create, the music that those words create. The words affect your mind, and the music goes directly to your heart."

Reading a book like *The Book of Mirdad* is an art by itself. Osho tells us, "And it is a book to be read by the heart, not by the mind. It is a book not to be understood, but experienced. It is something phenomenal. Millions of people have tried to write books so that they can express the inexpressible, but they have utterly failed. I know only one book, *The Book of Mirdad*, which has not failed; and if you cannot get to the very essence of it, it will be your failure, not the author's. He has created a perfect device of words, parables, situations. If you allow it, the book becomes alive and something starts happening to your being."

Mikhail Naimy writes, "You are the tree of life. Beware of fractioning yourselves. Set not a fruit against a fruit, a leaf against a leaf, a bough against a bough; nor set the stem against the roots; nor set the tree against the mother-soil. That is precisely what you do, when you love one part more than the rest or to the exclusion of the rest."

Our life functions in an organic connectivity. We are one life — and this life itself is godliness. While we are creating conflict constantly, living in man-made divisions of religions, races and nations, a man of meditation comes to realize that there exist no divisions and fractions in life. All divisions exist only in the over-developed heads and under-developed hearts of people. We are conscious of the leaves, branches and stems of the tree, but we cannot see the roots of the tree, the source of one life. This is the real misery of men on earth.

"No love is love that subjugates the lover. No love is love that draws a woman to a man only to breed more women and men and thus perpetuate their bondage to the flesh," writes Naimy.

Those who can see neither before nor after believe this segment of eternity to be itself eternity. They cling to the delusion of duality not knowing that the rule of life is unity.

# Balance your Budget:
# Reach in, Reach out

Sadhu Vishwamurtidas

he best of countries and corporations are so because they have the best of budgets. It is natural therefore, that many people are concerned about our national budget. But if they spent as much time worrying about their domestic budget as they did about the national one, the world would be a far better place. People remain glued to their television sets for hours, listening carefully to the budget speech. They spend even more time criticizing it afterwards. But very few focus inwards to analyse how exactly they have budgeted their own hard-earned money.

Many of us continue to spend well beyond our income, inviting debts and sometimes bankruptcy. That's why Bhagwan Swaminarayan advises in his *Shikshapatri*, "One should keep a daily record of one's expenditure and income and should always live within one's means. All of us, whether rich or poor, should give something to charity." This is practical, grassroots budgeting.

Still fewer people have worked out a 'life' budget for themselves. A life budget includes committing time to self, family, society and God. The lives of those who do this become richer — not just financially, but also socially and spiritually. Just as a country's budget must be well-balanced for its economy to be healthy, life's budget too has to be well-balanced for life to be lived fruitfully.

Many corporate executives invest all their time and effort in pursuing their careers and climbing the professional ladder. When they reach the summit, however, most realize it wasn't really worth all the toil. They discover that their victory is empty and that they won it at an irreparable loss to their health, family and psyche: Incurring obesity, heart disease and fatigue on the physiological front; separated spouse, estranged children and uncared for parents on the familial front; frustration, depression and stress on the physio-psychological front. In the US, Canada, China and Japan, this phenomenon has resulted in a tragic burgeoning of suicides and cardiovascular and cancer-related deaths. The Royal Bank of Canada devoted one of its monthly letters to this problem with the title, 'Let's Slow Down.' "We are victims of mounting tension," it enunciated. "We have difficulty relaxing: We are not living fully."

For many in India too, life has taken on these contours, and living it is rather like going downhill in a truck without brakes. But it is still not too late. The World Health Organization predicts that stress will be the Number One killer in the world by 2020. And stress is usually nothing more than an individual's failure to balance his lifestyle. Living life in a healthy manner and living it fully means we have to maintain regular food habits and follow a sensible diet, regular exercise and rest, going out with family, working for charity and spending time in self-reflection, meditation and prayer.

There is only one way to survive overwork or burnout: Be brave and bail out or you will be a loser. Life's rat race only produces losers. It has no winners. Even if it does, the winner is still a rat. And usually a very large one. A great sage asked a prosperous king, "If you were about to die of thirst and starvation and someone offered you a glass of water and a loaf of bread in exchange for your wealth and kingdom, would you give them to him?"

"Of course, I would," replied the king. "Anybody would."

"Then why," asked the sage, "have you wasted your entire life amassing all this land and wealth when they are worth no more to you than a glass of water and a loaf of bread?"

Consider deeply the value of your life. In the US, compensation for an injured knee is approximately $200,000. Then what to say for a damaged brain, injured eye, amputated leg, broken marriage or a mental breakdown? No price can be put on these things. What price, then, can we put on the entire, fully functioning human body?

Human life is priceless. God has bequeathed this limitless treasure trove to all. And as diversification is one of the secrets to successful investment, so is it the secret to a joyous and blessed life. Reach into your soul, and reach out to your family, society and God. Budget well.

# Take a Fresh Look at Patriotism

## MPK Kutty

anuary 23, is the birth anniversary of Netaji Subash Chandra Bose. It is also observed as the National Day of Patriotism. "In the name of God, I take this sacred oath that to liberate India and 380 million of my countrymen, I, Subash Chandra Bose, will continue the sacred war of freedom till the last breath of my life. I shall remain the servant of India and to look after the welfare of 380 million of Indian brothers and sisters shall be for me my highest duty" — this was Netaji's oath of allegiance to India after proclaiming the establishment of the provisional government of India at a cinema hall in Singapore on October 21, 1942.

Though Bose chose a path so distinct from Gandhi's, the Mahatma made this observation about him: "The greatest lesson we can draw from Netaji's life is the way in which he infused the spirit of unity amongst his men so that they could rise above all religious and provincial barriers and shed together their blood for the common cause."

Today patriotism is a much-debated value, the protagonists and antagonists resorting to their own narrow interpretations. Rabindranath Tagore had a more enlightened view of nationalism. His treatise on nationalism is being studied in British universities. Generally, nationalism is inextricably linked with patriotism. In his book, *Nationalism,* Tagore says that nationalism is an invention of the West. The nation has thrived for long upon mutilated humanity. Society increasingly has become a marionette show of politicians, soldiers, manufacturers and bureaucrats.

"Nationalism is a great menace. It is the particular thing which for years has been at the bottom of India's troubles," wrote Tagore, much before the country won independence; much before it witnessed partition and the ensuing bloodbath or the genesis of the Kashmir issue. Where the spirit of nationalism prevails the people are being taught from childhood to hate the 'enemy'.

Tagore sees in nationalism, instincts of self-aggrandizement of whole peoples organized together with all the paraphernalia of power and prosperity, its flags and hymns and patriotic bragging. Nations are engaged in a wrestling match; they are not bound to listen to the voice of truth and goodness.

Writing in a similar vein, Earl Stanley Jones, a visionary and close associate of Mahatma Gandhi wrote: "One of the greatest dangers to world peace is the rise of modern nationalism. It has taken that lovely sentiment called patriotism and has turned it into the deadliest enemy known to the modern world. It causes men to sin where they otherwise would not."

The common people of own nation usually have no reason to hate the common people of another nation. But nationalism takes hold of these common people, subjects them to propaganda, instils fear, inspires hate, puts bayonets into their hands and flings them against the common people of another country. The grinning devil inspires this mad business called nationalism.

"The time is fast approaching when to call a man a patriot will be the deepest insult you can offer him," — so begins Count Leo Tolstoy, writing an essay on patriotism as early as in the year 1900. The feeling of patriotism, he wrote, 'is unnatural, irrational and harmful' and a cause of great part of the ills afflicting mankind. So far from being a virtue, as virulently projected by certain sections in politics here, the prophet in Tolstoy saw it as an undesirable emotion, to be overcome by all means available to rational man.

The willingness to kill or sacrifice peace and property in defence of one's land and people was an ideal when it was considered just to plunder and kill people of other nations. But as nations and individuals evolved from lower to higher ideas, outmoded customs got discarded. The progress of civilization saw the abolition of slavery, for instance. The trend towards globalization should enable nations to relate to one another in the new idiom. Perhaps Tolstoy's prophetic warning about patriotism being a source of much evil needs to be taken seriously.

# Parable of the King & the Poet-thief

Sudhamahi Regunathan

ight was falling. The moon was playing hide and seek with the clouds. The trees were swaying with a gentle breeze. The king looked out of the window of his palace. His city seemed to be in deep slumber. He settled down in his bed but try as he might, he could not fall asleep. When one cannot fall asleep, one's mind starts wandering. The king found himself thinking about his life. "What do I not have?" thought the king as he calculated his assets. He had everything.

He enumerated all that he was blessed with and found himself composing a verse: "Queens of unrivalled beauty and law-abiding citizens. Men of unparalleled sincerity and soft-spoken servants. Armies of trumpeting elephants and wind-paced horses."

All sleep vanished from the king's eyes. He needed one more line to complete the verse. So what if he had all this, how was he going to tie them up? What was the last line to be? Tossing and turning, the poet-king fell into what is called 'artistic angst'.

He repeated the first three lines a thousand times in the hope that the fourth may flow from them. His queens were beautiful, perhaps the most beautiful women that had ever been born. They all loved him. The people of his kingdom loved him. They supported him and stood by him at all times. His courtiers and friends were helpful and there was never any dissension just for the sake of it. And his army? The king swelled with pride. His strong majestic elephants could win any war on their own. He had horses that were unmatched in speed. Thus his army was one of the strongest ever. But what should the fourth line be? The king was now getting agitated.

In the king's city lived an impoverished poet. That night, he couldn't sleep because he was hungry. Searching for food, he sneaked into the king's palace. Groping his way in the dark, he found he had walked into the king's chamber. Sensing that the king was awake, the poet-thief sat down and moved as close to the ground as possible. Soon he reached the king's cot and lay underneath it. He saw a bowl of fruit on the table opposite the king's bed and decided to wait for the king to fall asleep so that he could get hold of the fruit. The hungry poet waited for a long time, but the king only tossed and turned. Finally, the poet paid attention to what the king was saying. Upon hearing the first three lines of the king's verse, he said, "I have them all which turn to nothing when the eye closes."

The words had slipped out spontaneously from the poet's mouth and only later did he realize his mistake. The king, excited on hearing the concluding line of his verse, jumped out of bed and looked around for the source of the voice. In just a single line, the voice had estimated the value of all that the king had. Beautiful and precious the king's possessions were, no doubt, but they were not eternal. They were guests of time.

The poet-thief was caught. "So, you are a thief," said the king, unsure of how to react.

"No sir," said the poet.

"I am not a thief. I am a poet. Poverty has made me steal." Indeed, reflected the king, paucity can mar character. He gave the poet a lakh gold coins and bid him farewell with respect.

Acharya Mahaprajna draws many lessons from this simple story. The idea of possessiveness is crippling. It leads to greed, arrogance, anger, aversion, fear and lust. These emotions are the seeds of violence and when they sprout, ugly incidents like fundamentalist violence take place. This does not mean one should give up possessions. It only means that one should give up possessiveness. Says the Acharya, "Both paucity and plenty are related to the idea of possessiveness and therefore mar character. Possessiveness could be of material wealth or of one's own beliefs and learning. True learning lies in accepting and appreciating another's also. True living is in sharing and practising amity."

Right conduct, right knowledge and right vision combined with intuition have to be developed to live a life of equanimity and bring peace to one's surroundings.

# Time to Rebuild Trust & Faith

## MPK Kutty

he danger of getting drawn into competition is that one will stoop low somewhere along the line to get the better of a rival, be it in business or when seeking a promotion. When pitted against petty people, you begin to think that you have to act at their level. You eventually adopt the world's ways and get cast in its mould.

Your determination to live up to your principles does not ensure that you will do so. People take to shortcuts believing that the path of goodness is strewn with pitfalls. Their argument is that we live in a cruel world where doing good simply does not pay.

They even give the example of Christ, saying that he went about healing people and teaching them how to attain eternal life.

Where did he end up? On the cross. This might be so, but it must not turn us away from doing good under all circumstances. As St Paul wrote to his friends in Galatia, "Let us not be weary in well doing; for in due season we shall reap, if we faint not." (Galatians 6:9 - Bible).

Motivational speaker Shiv Khera often stresses the fact that it is enough for good people to be indifferent for the wicked to succeed. A recent news item reported the discovery of the author of a popular maxim that pertains to 'being decent in a mean world'. According to the report, Kent M Keith, a Rhodes scholar, had written what have come to be known as 'paradoxical maxims' as a student at Harvard University 34 years ago. You might have come across these paradoxical commandments in many a home or office. They are, "People are unreasonable, illogical and self-centred. Love them anyway. If you do good, people will accuse you of selfish, ulterior motives; do good anyway. If you are successful, you will win false friends and true enemies.

Succeed anyway. The good you do will be forgotten tomorrow; do good anyway. Honesty and frankness make you vulnerable. Be honest and frank anyway.

"People favour underdogs; but follow only top dogs. Fight for some underdogs anyway. What you spend years building may be destroyed overnight; build anyway. People may need help but may attack you if you help them. Help people anyway. Give the world the best you have and you will get kicked in the teeth. Give the world the best you have got."

It is this way of thinking that gets eroded in the urban situation. For instance, you don't like your neighbour. He gets on your nerves. Or he does not reciprocate. The paradoxical maxims would still want us to go on extending a hand of friendship to him.

So too the Biblical message of Jesus. If you love only those who love you, lend only to those who lend to you, you are no better than sinners who do likewise, observed Jesus. He prescribed an active feeling of benevolence towards the other person, no matter how the other person reacts. And then he went on to advise to love those who hate you, to be kind to the thankless and the wicked; to pray for those who despised you, and so on.

Technology and science have created neighbours; but they have not ensured the brotherhood of men. This role should be taken on by religion. Religion, wrote Edmund Burke, is the basis of civil society and the source of good and comfort. But the spectacle enacted during Gujarat's communal violence does not reflect this at all. There were several acts of heroism in which people tried to come to the aid of their neighbours of another faith under attack. But there were also cases of indifference and active collusion in spreading violence.

In this scenario, to rebuild trust and faith among communities, it is necessary to foster the love-thy-neighbour philosophy. Never mind the colour, creed or language of your neighbour. You need him and he needs you. In times of crisis, neighbours prove to be more helpful than relatives, who might not be at hand.

Every religion teaches us to love our neighbour, and promotion of good neighbourliness is one way of enriching life and ensuring security. The ultimate message of the paradoxical commandments is the wisdom of being a good neighbour to a fellow being, regardless of returns.

# Right Karma Brings Freedom from Fear

Brahma Kumari Asha

ear seems to have taken possession of almost everyone in today's world and has become the biggest stress-producer. Fear lies in the subconscious and surfaces as and when a situation arises: of possible or imminent loss of life, property, loved ones or prestige, for example. The greatest fear of all is, of course, that of death, because all physical relationships and material possessions are lost with death. The fear of death, it is said, is worse than death itself.

What people fear most is untimely death, and this fear is growing because of the increasing uncertainties of life today. Scientific advances have made life more comfortable in many ways. However, insecurity has also kept pace with progress. Today everyone feels vulnerable, for anything can happen to anyone, anytime, anywhere. Our increasing tendency to violence and the growing mechanisation of our lives have created conditions in which death is just a careless moment away.

One reason for this insecurity is that more and more innocent people are getting killed in human-made situations, which may not even be of the victims' making. While we do get reconciled to the death of innocents in natural calamities or accidents by telling ourselves that it was willed by fate or that it was beyond our control, acts of wanton killing carried out by humans often leave a deep scar within us because they shake our trust in our fellow human beings.

Medical science has not yet found a cure for fear. Actually, it is a malady of the soul and calls for a spiritual solution. First of all, it requires an attitudinal change. We need to drill into our minds that one only loses by giving in to fear. It paralyses the mind, rendering it incapable of doing what it can easily do otherwise. The behaviour of pigeons illustrates this well. Frozen with fear when they see a cat, pigeons just shut their eyes instead of flying away. The result? They get killed. By practising to take on any situation calmly and with courage, we will be able to change our tendency to get frightened by unexpected or adverse circumstances.

Another change needed is in the way we look at adversity. All the tests that we face in life, regardless of whether we pass them or not, make us stronger and equip us to face better similar tests in future. If we dodge these tests for fear of failure or loss we will advance in life no more than a student who refuses to sit for examinations out of examination phobia.

The illusion of mortality is the deep rooted cause of fear. It stems from a wrong identification of the eternal self with the perishable body. It can be overcome by the realization of a basic truth: that we are souls and the soul is immortal. This is the first lesson of the *Bhagavad Gita*. The soul is an actor and the body is like its costume. It takes rebirth, casting off one body to take birth in a new body. What we call death is nothing but the departure of the soul from the body after its role in the present body is over. This is not an esoteric truth just to be wondered at, anyone can realize it by practising meditation. Living in soul-consciousness over a long period empowers us to overcome the fear of mortality. While attitudinal change can help us overcome fear to some extent, complete freedom from it requires attention on our karma.

Fear is always about the future but its roots lie in the past. It is the law of karma that we reap as we sow. Fear is punishment for our sins small and big. This is why some people are gripped by fear in a situation which others take lightly. The seemingly baseless and even peculiar fears or phobias that people suffer from — fear of the dark, fear of water, fear of going out alone, fear of certain places — are all in some manner influenced by past actions and experiences.

Our mythology eulogises the brave: the story of the doughty monkey prince, Angad, the emissary of Rama, standing his own in the court of Ravana is well known, and Durga, the eight-armed female deity who rides a lion, symbolizes feminine courage and power. It is with such courage that countless martyrs braved death and great men like Mahatma Gandhi overcame seemingly insurmountable odds.

# Patanjali's Guide to Self-evolution

By Nidhesh Gupta

atanjali's Yoga Sutra forms the basis of all yoga that is practised today. It contains knowledge which is useful for all, whether one is an evolved yogi, a developing *sadhaka* or an uninitiate. In the astanga yoga, the eight constituents of yoga are discussed. Of these, the first constituent talks of the five *yama*. These are the restraints every human being is advised to practise in day-to-day living.

The first yama is related to *ahimsa* or non-violence, not only in action, but also in thought, in speech and in every other conceivable way. The 35th yoga sutra of the Sadhana Pada says that when one practises non-violence, then, others too would give up hostilities in one's presence.

The second *yama, satya,* requires one to be truthful, sincere and honest. Truthfulness is to be practised by all, irrespective of what stage of spiritual evolution they may be at. In the 36th yoga sutra, Patanjali promises that when you practise truth, your words will have so much power that they would fructify and bear fruit.

The third *yama, asteya,* says that one shall not steal. The 37th yoga sutra promises that the one who abstains from stealing, will obtain *sarvaratna*. The promise made by the sage is that as a man abstains from stealing, precious things would begin to come his way. The promise is not just for materially precious things; it is also for qualities of value.

The fourth *yama, brahmacharya,* does not require complete abstinence, as is commonly thought. Sage Vasishta considered himself to be a *brahmachari* even though he had hundred children. It is only when one indulges in sexual activity for purely physical purposes that *brahmacharya* is compromised. In the 38th yoga sutra of the Sadhana Pada the sage talks about the *labha* or gain for one who practises *brahmacharya*.

The fifth *yama, aparigraha,* requires us to give up greed. It relates to non-covetousness. It can also be interpreted as having no extra possessions. There is thus a free flow of all that comes in and goes out. The 39th yoga sutra promises that for such a one, knowledge of the past and also of the future would be known.

Interestingly, we can draw parallels between these five *yama* and The Ten Commandments believed to have been given by God to Moses on Mount Sinai. The following commandments correspond to the five *yama*: Thou shall not kill. Thou shall not bear false witness against thy neighbour. Thou shall not steal. Thou shall not commit adultery. Thou shall not covet thy neighbour's house, thou shall not covet thy neighbour's wife, nor his manservant, nor his maidservant, nor any thing that is thy neighbour's.

These simple principles which are mentioned in Patanjali's Yoga Sutras, as well as in the Bible, provide the foundation on which every human being can evolve through introspection. It is easy to condemn others for not practising these principles, whilst completely overlooking one's own limitations in this respect.

The Bible narrates how when some Jews brought to Jesus a woman who had committed adultery, he said, "He that is without sin among you, let him cast stones upon her." One by one, all those who were gathered there left. Left alone with the woman, Jesus asked her, "Where are thine accusers? Hath no man condemned thee?"

She replied, "No man, my Lord."

Jesus said, "Neither do I condemn thee: Go, and sin no more."

The practice of the Ten Commandments, as also of the moral injunctions set out in the five *yama* are meant to be applied to oneself — they are not for purposes of passing judgment on others. These principles can be followed as guidelines for laying the foundation for one's spiritual evolution.

# Life is too Precious to be Squandered

Cyrus H Merchant

his morning, work took me to a place where little children and old people were lying on the floor — an unreal heat, an unreal poverty, but very real people. Three little children like little broken Christs or broken Krishnas (I couldn't tell their religion) condemned to a life the old around them were probably waiting to end.

And this evening as I stood in the Fire Temple, I wondered, would they ever know the privilege of finishing a good day with a good bath and a good hour of worship?

All prosperity, like all joy, is a gift of God. But people take these blessings for granted. Worse, they squander them throughout their lives. You don't know when life will end; yet, you are unwilling to live life truthfully, in the company of God. You have God's blessings — you have a home, a happy heart, health.

From the Torah down to every other holy book, a way of life has been prescribed — not just a way of life, but the way of life, for, ultimately, there is only one way. But not everyone prays every day. I would really like to know, how many adults even thank the elements — earth, water, air, fire — or the Provider? If you are one of the blessed, ask yourself, are you leading your life the way God would want you to? Your heart will give you the answer in a second. If you were one of those for whom a kitchen sink, leave alone a kitchen, is an unattainable luxury, what would you be doing with your life? Pretty much nothing. Poverty, illiteracy and misery are iron chains. Forget doing something, you can't even dream. Even a day is far from being perfect.

But for the rest of us life is near perfect, we have more than we need to have. But does this stir or inspire you to take that leap towards a perfect life? If you don't begin today, then when will you begin? Are you allowing your life to fool you? Your mind will play tricks, it will let you believe what you want, but when you go to your heart it will tell you what an illness, tragedy, upheaval usually does — it will tell you that you aren't happy.

There is an abnormal amount of apathy towards real living. What a waste of life! All the small things have become attractive, the big things are cast aside, as if they belong only to the scriptures or some forgotten time when people worshipped a God who gave openly. You have it all but you squander it all. Worse, you hanker after things that are transitory; things which won't last.

In our cities, people's lifestyles have become like a gravy that has congealed. It makes me physically ill. The definition of what works for those following this sick lifestyle is so much at variance with that of those aspiring to a life lived by God's definition. I am unable to be around people or places where the beauty of blessings — and their benevolent Provider — is not present, or welcome.

I have an inner reluctance towards anything that departs from the simple and special things of life. I am compelled to withdraw. Never mind who or what it might be — if he/it doesn't put a gleam in God's eye, he/it is mere dust. From dust, of dust, belonging to dust.

Success is no measure, because these days just about anything is successful. Neither is happiness a measure, because these days even the most twisted things make people happy. Things are far from being perfect. Therefore, sometimes you do go down; but at least, go down fighting for what is right. And, for what is really lasting.

# Nehru's Letter to Children in India

Jawaharlal Nehru

Dear Children,

I like being with children and talking to them and, even more, playing with them. For the moment I forget that I am terribly old and it is very long ago since I was a child. But when I sit down to write, I cannot forget my age and the distance that separates you from me. Old people have a habit of delivering sermons and good advice to the young.

I remember that I disliked this very much long ago when I was a boy. So I suppose you do not like it very much either. Grown-ups also have a habit of appearing to be very wise, even though very few of them possess much wisdom. I have not yet quite made up my mind whether I am wise or not. Sometimes listening to others I feel that I must be wise and brilliant and important. Then, looking at myself, I begin to doubt this. In any event, people who are wise do not talk about their wisdom and do not behave as if they were very superior persons...

What then shall I write about? If you were with me, I would love to talk to you about this beautiful world of ours, about flowers, trees, birds, animals, stars, mountains, glaciers and all the other beautiful things that surround us in the world. We have all this beauty all around us and yet we, who are grown-ups, often forget about it and lose ourselves in our arguments or in our quarrels. We sit in our offices and imagine that we are doing very important work.

I hope you will be more sensible and open your eyes and ears to this beauty and life that surrounds you. Can you recognize the flowers by their names and the birds by their singing? How easy it is to make friends with them and with everything in nature, if you go to them affectionately and with friendship. You must have read many fairy tales and stories of long ago. But the world itself is the greatest fairy tale and story of adventure that was ever written. Only we must have eyes to see and ears to hear and a mind that opens out to the life and beauty of the world.

Grown-ups have a strange way of putting themselves in compartments and groups. They build barriers of religion, caste, colour, party, nation, province, language, customs and of rich and poor. Thus they live in prisons of their own making.

Fortunately, children do not know much about these barriers, which separate. They play and work with each other and it is only when they grow up that they begin to learn about these barriers from their elders. I hope you will take a long time in growing up. Some months ago, the children of Japan wrote to me and asked me to send them an elephant. I sent them a beautiful elephant on behalf of the children of India. This noble animal became a symbol of India to them and a link between them and the children of India. I was very happy that this gift of ours gave so much joy to so many children of Japan, and made them think of our country. Remember that everywhere there are children like you going to school and work and play, and sometimes quarrelling but always making friends again. You can read about these countries in your books, and when you grow up many of you will visit them. Go there as friends and you will find friends to greet you.

You know we had a very great man amongst us. He was called Mahatma Gandhi. But we used to call him affectionately Bapuji. He was wise, but he did not show off his wisdom. He was simple and childlike in many ways and he loved children. He taught us to face the world cheerfully and with laughter.

Our country is a very big country and there is a great deal to be done by all of us. If each one of us does his or her little bit, then all this mounts up and the country prospers and goes ahead fast. I have tried to talk to you in this letter as if you were sitting near me, and I have written more than I intended.

Chacha Nehru,
December 3, 1949

# A Responsive Life

## Homayun Taba

wo young crew-members survived an airplane crash several years ago; each came out with a different inference. One felt that she had come so close to death, and this unsettling experience might happen again, that she shut a door on life. The second said that if death could be so close at hand, then a window must be opened — life demands a more zestful engagement and a fuller meaning.

As a matter of fact, the key word here is 'meaning'. As human beings, we live with a far more complex process of meaning-assigning or meaning-deriving than any other creature.

This is because we can rise beyond instinctual programming to exercise choice, take up roles and change the course of our lives. We are also capable of taking our own life if we felt it had 'no meaning'.Our meaning-assigning process, which is closely connected with the mental models we hold, gives us more freedom — but it can often turn us into prisoners of our own programming. Even the most 'educated' among us reveal, upon inquiry, assumptions that are derived from narrow meanings or unverified meanings that are strongly adhered to; we often work from 'realities' that are more imaginary constructions than truly experienced realities. Social psychologists describe this as the act of giving 'frozen meanings' to events and relationships.

Identity, for some of us, is so linked with our work, position, status, that often on retirement we find our existence fraught with feelings of meaninglessness. Realistically, our new life-location demands a new set of responses and a fresh look at priorities to keep our identity and selfhood intact. But to arrive at the insight that identity can pick up or give up roles, needs a capability that comes from constant examination of one's mental models and the ability to dissolve frozen meanings.

Therefore, the need to sift through and discard what does not add to our wholesomeness and well-being. Someone described this as:

Not looking back in anger or forward in fear, but around in awareness. This constitutes a life of constant redefinitions and renewals.

Our growth path will eventually bring us face to face with moments when we need to break boundaries, to examine meanings that have been given to us, and which we have deeply internalized. As part of this process of discovering our 'personhood' we need to penetrate each layer of doubt that lies beneath each surface of certainty handed down to us by our families and cultures.

Coming out of the trials and tribulations, we might get a glimpse of what it would be like to think and act, not out of the limitations of entrenched beliefs and limited meanings, but out of choices and preferences — to live in grace and with authenticity.

As one's focus moves from the psycho-social to the psycho-spiritual realm, new revelations unfold. Here, the core identity is repeatedly identified with or reminded of its connectedness, in essence, with the Transcendent. This is shown in allegorical literature as a state of being in exile, hence the search for reconnection, or flowing back into the ocean.

In every spiritual tradition, the meaning-assigning process assumes deeper connections between the outer and the inner worlds. Nature is seen as mother, sacredness finds relevance in the most mundane object, and every intention and ensuing action becomes a significant strand in weaving the fabric of ultimate liberation. Every symbol, every ritual, though enacted on earth is said to reflect a divine prototype.

Any soul concerned with 'questions of ultimate concern' seeks to make meaning of his or her life, and of the lives around. Such a person also seeks to get beyond the gnawing feelings of futility and to come into a life that is truly 'meaningful'.

Our initial attempts gain momentum, become a search for those meanings from which we can act with courage and humanness. This can help us, each in our own way, to become vital persons — where we are able to relate to the lives around us, to replace barrenness with sumptuousness and to add significance and value to the systems in which we operate.

# A Teacher Who was Not Afraid to Learn

## Luis SR Vas

E ven in an age when the written word has yielded before the televisual image, certain books can revolutionize one's outlook on life. Father Anthony de Mello, the Indian Jesuit and writer who died 11 years ago, recounts one such incident in his book, *Contact with God*: "I was giving a conference to a group of sisters one evening and telling them how few are the books that really teach us to pray. That evening one of those sisters said to me, "I've discovered a book that deals exactly with the problem you mentioned. It teaches you in a practical way how to pray. Would you care to read it?"

Having begun to reading the book after supper, Fr de Mello found it so fascinating that he stayed up late into the night. Titled *The Way of A Pilgrim,* the book was discovered at the beginning of this century — in manuscript form, in the cell of a monk at Mount Athos after his death. It soon became a spiritual classic and was widely translated and is available in Hindi, Tamil, Malayalam and Marathi.

This is the story of a Russian pilgrim who wants to know how to pray without ceasing, and is in search of someone who will show him how to do this. One day, he finds a monk who tells him to repeat the prayer 'Lord Jesus Christ have mercy on me' in rhythm with his breathing, first five hundred times a day, then a thousand and so on.

Fr de Mello took up the practice: "Within less than a month I noticed that there was a marked change in my prayer. All I did was repeat this as often during the day as I remembered to, not only during the time of prayer but also at periods when I happened to be free, when I waited for a bus or a train or was walking from one place to another."

The change he experienced, Fr de Mello reports, was difficult to describe. "It was nothing sensational. I began to feel somewhat more peaceful, more recollected, more integrated — if that makes any sense: to feel a certain depth within me," he write. "I also noticed that the prayer had the habit of springing to my lips almost automatically anytime I was not occupied with some mental activity; then I would begin to repeat it, sometimes just mechanically, sometimes meaningfully."

Fr de Mello goes on to discuss the Jesus prayer, tying it up with the psychology of the unconscious and drawing parallels with the effects of reciting the rosary. The episode and its analysis is typical of Fr de Mello's approach to spirituality — the practicality, the thoroughness that distinguished everything he did.

His earliest book, *Sadhana*, drew heavily on the practice and insights of Vipassana meditation, which he studied with a Buddhist teacher; he also studied Zen Buddhism and was attracted to the teachings of Jiddu Krishnamurti. From these experiences emerged, not scholarly tomes of the kind that other Catholic scholars and divines have produced after their encounter with Eastern spirituality, but books like *The Song of the Bird, One-Minute Wisdom* and *The Prayer of the Frog*. These are collections of spiritual stories gathered from diverse traditions, countries and cultures; they are books written 'not to instruct but to Awaken'.

As Fr Parmananda Divarkar observed in his introduction to one of his books, Tony de Mello evolved as a being through three distinct stages: outwardly and in his relations with others, from spiritual director through therapist to guru; and inwardly, in his practice of the inner life, 'through a progression of values from holiness through love to freedom'.

In his last letter to a friend, written on the day before his death on June 2, 1987, Tony de Mello observed, "I find the whole of my interest is now focused on something else, on the 'world of the spirit', and I see everything else as trifling and so irrelevant... never before in my life have I felt so happy, so free."

# Striding Along a Path That is the Goal

## KB Rao

The phrase *Tat tvam asi* or 'That thou art', first uttered by Shvetaketu's father in the Chandogya Upanishad, had troubled me for years; and since I had acquired the status if not the wisdom of a senior citizen, this unease had taken on an urgency absent arlier. "Who am I?" and "Why am I here?" were just two of the questions for which I had no answers.

Numerous genes had gone into my 'I-ness'. Frustrated Michelangelos struggled with clumsy artisans, Oliviers with stuttering hams; here and there a Socrates who preferred coffee to hemlock vied with a Savonarola who kept his opinions to himself. Though I hadn't realized any of the many hopes, I had no regrets. It's true I hadn't set the Ganga or the local stream on fire, but life had been good.

Friends had called me a 'mere stick in the mud'. My reply was that that I was something more than that, a stick with aspirations to put forth leaves and flowers, and even to introspect. Like Shvetaketu, I had stripped the seed of the *nyagrodha* tree. He had been told that the 'nothingness' he found was the essence of the tree. I was forced to ask myself whether nothingness wasn't my essence too. My yesterdays were half-realized dreams, after all, and my tomorrows mere visions. Hence the nothingness of my todays made me sit up and take stock, as it were.

My browsing in the sacred books hadn't helped me to define my role or my relationship with God. Others more stupid than I had seen the essence, it seemed, while I perceived only nothingness. I was often tempted to cry: "O God, if there be a God, tell me about my soul, if I have one." Was it that I hadn't listened to God's call? Had I turned my back when He had beckoned?

Very early in life, I had realized that there was more to spiritual awakening than participating in rituals, reciting mantras or even meeting saintly persons. One's relationship with God was a very personal matter. It was in solitude that I had sought my God, and it was in that same solitude that I have had, at times, an infinitesimally tiny sense of being near Him, so small that I felt I was dreaming. A sunset, a view of mountains, the roar of the sea, or even the flash of the kingfisher's quick passage had made me feel His presence. Like many others, I too had received the sacred mantra.

It had, however, acted more as a sedative than as a conduit bringing holy thoughts. I wasn't experiencing God; nor was God, I felt, experiencing me.

Gautama needed the cycle of human misery to put him on the 'Way to Buddhahood'; a falling apple revealed a basic law of nature to Newton; and Archimedes only had to take a bath.

The message, when it came to me, wasn't conveyed by any guru. A few lines printed on a wrapper enclosing ready-made garments opened my eyes! They were from Emerson. I had at times taught selections from Emerson's work to my students, but hadn't felt the impact. Now his words seemed charged, as though they had in them the kernel of what Shvetaketu's father had called the 'essence'. And, in some odd way, they seemed to provide an answer to my questions.

The lines were: "To laugh often and much; to win the respect of intelligent people and the affection of children, to earn the appreciation of honest critics and endure the betrayal of false friends, to appreciate beauty; to find the best in others; to leave the world a bit better, whether by a healthy child, a garden path, or a redeemed social condition; to know even one life has breathed easier because you lived. This is to have succeeded."

In a strange way, these words had not only defined my purpose in life but also taught me how I could live it; and by making others happy, I could be happy myself and please God too in the bargain. Carpers might say that I am too easily satisfied, or that I am taking too much for granted. Who cares?

I have always believed in the little voice within, and it told me firmly that even though I might have missed all the buses, and taken all the low roads, I had still managed to find some favour in the eyes of my God.

# A Teacher Who Sang of Liberty & Enlightenment

MC Dinakaran

n this period of rampant sectarianism, it is of the first importance for us to remember the example set by modern mystics like Sri Narayana Guru, whose presence illuminated Kerala over the late 19th and early 20th centuries. This influential teacher emphasized, simultaneously, the importance of constructive social action and of inner transformation.

Narayana Guru emerged as an accomplished exponent of Vedanta at a crucial moment in Kerala's, and in India's, history. Shankara's Advaita vision — which had energized the subcontinent a millennium before — had receded. In its wake had arisen a society so preoccupied with the hierarchical need to grade and segregate humans from humans, that Swami Vivekananda was moved to describe Kerala, its most extreme example, as a 'madhouse'.

The maharajas and the Zamorin — who ruled the various states that formed the Kerala region — were bound in vassalage to the British Raj. As a result, the poor and depressed classes lived under two yokes: that of feudal casteism and that of exploitative colonialism.

It was in this ethos that Narayana Guru presented his new interpretation of Vedanta, which cut at the roots of the prevailing Brahminical orthodoxy.

Narayana Guru's corpus was disseminated in three languages: Sanskrit, Tamil and Malayalam. The hundred verses of his Darsana Mala, composed in Sanskrit, provide the seeker a careful analysis of the causes of this universe and of its foundational truth. The hundred verses of his Atmopadesa Satakam, composed in Malayalam, tell of the pleasures of the philosophically examined life.

On a superficial reading, Narayana Guru seems to dwell only on the bliss of the Infinite and has nothing to say about social reform or revolution. And yet, we must listen to his voice again.

An evolved soul, the Guru spent years in penance in the mountains and jungles of the Western Ghats; he wandered among the little-known *siddha ashrams* of the deep south. He could have lived in that state of bliss forever; but, as he sang in a famous *keertan* addressed to Lord Subrahmanya,

> "The clear moonlight fades, the sun has risen
> But wait a little before you merge with the Infinite.
> This is the time to help the helpless souls led astray
> To dive into the river of *Dharma!*"

The moonlight refers to the restless mind, the sun to realization; the stanza demonstrates the seeker's consciousness of his responsibility, his Bodhisattva-like awareness that he must remain in the world to help the last of mortals to achieve nirvana.

While quietly re-interpreting the first principles of Advaita in a modern egalitarian idiom, Narayana Guru also encouraged the Dalit masses — who had been denied the opportunity of refined education for centuries —to establish schools and workshops for themselves. His message was simple and potent, "Become enlightened by *vidya*; become strong through *sanghatana*".

The impact of Narayana Guru's message may be gauged from the fact that almost every community in Kerala (both Hindu and non-Hindu) has, in the last 75 years, set up colleges and other educational institutions of its own. This cultivation of consciousness has borne fruit in the high quality of life and education that Kerala enjoys today.

But Narayana Guru's greatest contribution was his rescue of Hinduism from its oppressive priestly class. He established temples where priests were not appointed on the basis of birth; he encouraged the low castes to abandon low forms of worship; he located the temples in beautiful surroundings and kept the sanctum sanctorum free of dirt. Even today, the cleanest of all Hindu temples are the ones founded by Narayana Guru. One has only to visit the Subrahmanya temple at Kovalam, the Sarada Temple at Varkala, or the Sree Sundareshwara Temple at Cannanore to confirm this.

Narayana Guru gave classical Advaita a fresh lease of life by shattering the philosophical basis of hierarchical Hinduism. He demolished the arguments of privilege by using the Vedantic concept of the oneness of all existence; humanity, he proclaimed, was one caste. At the same time — and most significantly — he ensured that antipathy towards the caste system did not degenerate into hatred for all upper-caste men and women.

Narayana Guru attracted disciples from all castes and communities; but, like all great souls, he was not succeeded by yogis of his calibre. His emancipatory impulse may have died out of the institutions he founded; but even so, Kerala as it exists today — a cosmopolitan society with relative communal amity and a high literacy rate — is a living monument to his work.

# Love as an Antidote
# to Negative Energy

Valson Thampu

wo affirmations are common to all religions. Every religion upholds peace as a supreme value; and every religion acknowledges love as the foremost attribute of God. Religions thus intuit a connection between love and peace. Divine love expresses itself as the blessing of peace in the sphere of creation.

In Christian thought Jesus who came to reveal God's love for the world is identified as the prince of peace. He urged his disciples to be peacemakers. Jesus made it clear that they were to pursue this spiritual vocation by creating a culture of love.

Almost all Hindu prayers end chanting peace — the threefold repetition of Om Shanti. Islam, as the name indicates, is a religion of peace. Jainism and Buddhism take the commitment to peace to exalted heights. The valorous opposition to the forces of evil in Sikhism stems from a basic commitment to peace and justice, as a measure of its moral vitality.

How do the resources of love become the logic of peace? To understand this, we have to note the fact and frontiers of love, understood spiritually and scripturally rather than romantically.

Love in the heart promotes relationship. Love is the cementing force between people. Those who are relationship-oriented prefer peace to conflict in their approach to others. On the contrary, those who are governed by hate are more at home in interpersonal conflict. They are bored by peace. At the macro-level, hate aggravates alienation between nations and provokes war and large-scale cruelty. It is when love dries up in religion that it succumbs to communalism and degenerates into an instrument of alienation.

In the mind, love becomes passion for truth. The love of truth, which includes the refusal to be enslaved by untruth, is integral to the commitment to peace. On the contrary, all war-efforts as well as ideologies of violence wield untruth as their choice weapon. The innate preference for peace in our ancient culture is embodied in the Vedic prayer: 'lead us from darkness to light, from untruth to truth, and from death to immortality'.

Darkness and death are the traditional symbols of untruth. It is love-inspired passion for truth that becomes the commitment to justice and righteousness. Justice is the essence of *dharma*, that which undergirds and sustains a society. *Dharma* is synonymous with peace. Peace is not merely the absence of war or conflict. It is a state of comprehensive well-being as indicated by the Jewish concept of Shalom.

Love in the soul finds its expression as compassion. Every religion celebrates compassion as a seminal spiritual virtue. It is the nourisher and refiner of our humanity. It is an attribute of God that finds its reflection in the human soul. The life of Ashoka the Great proves — if proof is required — that compassion eradicates war-mongering. Compassion is a pre-condition for peace. Even as a people abjure compassion in their culture and outlook, they acquire a taste for conflict and cruelty. Consequently, the craving for war robs peace of its attractiveness and desirability in their eyes. Where there is love there is willingness, even eagerness, to serve. The erosion of love cripples the spirit of service. Apathy turns service into boredom and hate corrupts it into an infliction. Work is sacred; but its sanctity can be experienced only in an ambiance of love. Service is more than work. It is an acknowledgement of our belonging together through the medium of work. Service is also a statement of our attitude to others.

Murder and destruction are also works; works inspired by demonic hate. War baptizes service in the cult of violence. Spirituality orientates service to peace and progress.

Love, as it nourishes a society, becomes the natural climate — the plausibility structure — for peace. It is impossible to create a culture of peace without nurturing in people a capacity and commitment to love. This is the spiritual standpoint. The worldly assumption, in contrast, holds that peace results from the balance of terror. By this logic, the invincibility of wars leads to peace. When the nations of the world know that there are no victors in wars, peace will prevail in the world. However, the millions of lives lost since World War II and the many conflicts that continue to ravage peoples in the Afro-Asian nations disprove this assumption.

The world's quest for peace is shaped by the paradigm of power which also, ironically, shapes its approach to war. That is why peace remains an interlude between wars, and not a stable condition for human life and well-being. The Indian contribution to the discourse of peace must focus on the spiritual foundations of the culture of peace.

From a spiritual perspective, it is obvious that peace cannot be pursued as a goal in itself. Peace is a holistic phenomenon. That is to say, it can be realized only if all its coordinates — relationship, truth, justice, compassion, service and development — are also nurtured and affirmed. This calls for a paradigm shift from the culture of power to the culture of love. Hence the spiritual correlation between the culture of peace and the culture of love.

# Uses of Spirituality
# at the Workplace

R Venkatesan

oes the recent interest exhibited in non-fiction titles such as *The Soul of Business, A Spiritual Audit of Corporate America, The Stirring of Soul in the Workplace, The Three-Minute Meditation* etc, in the US point to the possible evolution of the 'enlightened corporate sector'? Do Indian managers, born in a land that has offered 'yoga and meditation' to the world corporate sector (to overcome stress), have the 'first-mover advantage'? These are the questions that should interest 'enlightened' managers in 'progressive' Indian corporations.

Regardless of the size of a firm, much of the work is accomplished by people working together as a team. During the 1970s and 1980s, Japanese firms recognized the virtues of team work over individualistic style of functioning. Thus arose the concept of a 'team' — a cohesive group with well-defined objectives — where each member had a specific role to play.

However, the Japanese found the task of balancing group ethos with individual drive and motivation a difficult task and had to selectively promote the concepts of 'individualistic' engineers, and a general flexibility for members to move across teams, to nurture the entrepreneurial talent within the organisational umbrella.

Apart from 'motivational' aspects in different cultural settings, another important behaviour that has gained attention is 'stress'. International research on stress related factors has found that while Swedish executives experience the least stress, executives from the US, UK and the former West Germany are able to manage the stress effectively unlike their counterparts in Japan, Singapore, Brazil, Egypt, South Africa and Nigeria.

Both *Newsweek* and *Time* have recently devoted special articles to stress and stress busters. The common theme has been that chronic stress is harmful to both employees and employers and that the solution lies in the ancient Indian practice of yoga and meditation. Yoga as the union between the mind and body is seen to offer solutions to stress related problems, which the physical workouts/exercise cannot offer. Not to be outdone, numerous titles and solutions related to spirituality, all home grown, have appeared on the scene.

The recent work of Danah Zohar on spiritual intelligence, John Kay on implicit or trust relations within the firm and between the firm and its stakeholders and Avinash K Dixit on the science of strategic thinking point out future directions for the corporate sector.

Zohar refers to spiritual intelligence — a form of creative thinking which is concerned as much with rule making as rule breaking — as the basic foundation for an effective emotional quotient (EQ) and IQ. She says that SQ could be explained in terms of the lotus model with its centre and six petals, corresponding to the seven *chakras* described by the Hinduism's Kundalini Yoga. According to Kay, the essence of a firm is defined by the totality of relationships among, first, its stakeholders and, second, between itself and other firms. This unique structure of formal and informal relationships, which cannot be easily replicated, is the real source of a firm's competitive advantage in the marketplace.

Dixit mentions that unlike a traditional firm which tries to 'hold' rather than 'share' information, a progressive and enlightened firm makes sharing its dominant strategy.

According to *Time's* special article on Yoga, 'enlightenment and good health require a proper balance between the seven major *chakras* apart from a free flow of the life force which, in turn, is acquired through awakening of dormant Kundalini energy.' The Indian philosophical tradition attributes perception to the mind, conceptualization to the intellect and 'illumination' to the self. Further, they speak of an ascent from 'intellect' through meditation. The integration of inner self with the cosmic spirit — otherwise, referred to self-realization — is considered the route to highest knowledge. In other words, spirituality at the workplace is considered necessary not only in terms of managing stress but also as an aid in reaching higher levels of consciousness.

Mataji Shri Nirmala Devi, the founder of Sahaja Yoga, says, "En masse inner transformation of human beings by self-realization is the reality now. Everyone can now become aware of the absolute truth and reality through Sahaja Yoga. Sahaja Yoga is the spontaneous union of individual consciousness with the all-pervading power through the awakening of the residual power of the *kundalini* which lies dormant within all human beings in the triangular bone at the base of the spine, called the sacrum — the sacred bone."

Perhaps it is time for Indian corporates to draw upon the great traditions of India's ancient spiritual and  philosophical heritage.